L. H. MYERS

A CRITICAL STUDY

BY

G. H. BANTOCK

Reader in Education
in the University College of Leicester

UNIVERSITY COLLEGE
LEICESTER
AND
JONATHAN CAPE
THIRTY BEDFORD SQUARE, LONDON
1956

Printed by Sir Isaac Pitman & Sons, Ltd.
at the Pitman Press, Bath, England
for the
Publications Board
University College, Leicester
and
Jonathan Cape
Thirty Bedford Square, London

LEO MYERS

TO MY WIFE

PREFACE

IN its original form, this book was considerably longer, the biographical section equalling in length the critical. For reasons of expense in publication, the former has been drastically cut to about a sixth of its original length. I cannot say I much regret the enforced pruning. What seem to me the important things in Myers's development I have managed to retain, though much of the evidence on which they have been based has had to be erased. It was, in any case, impossible to present a full picture of the man with the evidence available. What happened to Leo Myers was chiefly domestic and private. He entered little into the public eye; he took no part in journalism; he never broadcast. Before his suicide he destroyed all copies of his autobiography and urged his friends to burn any letters they had received from him, which a number of them did. He was not, anyhow, a very good letter writer—as he himself remarked: "What I have I have put into my books." Most of those I have been privileged to see have been of a social or semi-philosophical nature; others, for acceptable personal reasons, have been denied to me. The full details of his private life cannot, in any case, yet be told. Nor can I think it very important for purely critical purposes that they should. What matters about a writer is what he had to say; "never trust the artist, trust the tale," as Lawrence puts it.

I am deeply indebted to the late Mrs Elsie Myers and other members of Myers's family for their assistance with information, and to a number of Myers's friends, many of whom are mentioned in the text of the book, for biographical material. In particular, the late Olaf Stapledon was a constant source of assistance and kindly encouragement. I would also like to thank Professor A. R. Humphreys and Mr P. A. W. Collins of the University College of Leicester, and Professor A. K. Croston of the University College of the West Indies, for having read through the text and made suggestions for improvement. I am most grateful to the Publications Board of the University College of Leicester for undertaking the publication of the book and to its secretary, Dr G. B. Pyrah, for his help in preparing the manuscript for the press. I would acknowledge the generosity of Myers's trustees and of Messrs Putnam and Jonathan Cape for allowing me to quote from the novels. Thanks are also due to Sir John Rothenstein and Mr Michael Rothenstein for permission to reproduce the drawing by Sir William Rothenstein which appears as frontispiece. Finally, my thanks are due to my wife for having undertaken the ungrateful task of numerous re-typings and for her sustained critical interest in the development of the book.

G. H. B.

University College,
Leicester
June, 1955

CONTENTS

CHAPTER I

"THE ORISSERS"

I T is a commonplace that one of the main efforts of the intellectual during the last hundred and fifty years has been that of integration, of arriving at some *modus vivendi* with both the forces of society and more transcendental powers. The break-up of the eighteenth-century social order, following the Industrial Revolution, was accompanied by a reaction against its over-rationalised philosophic outlook. The force of the irrational was recognised by the romantic writers, who, looking outwards and finding much that was unacceptable, were forced to seek 'inspiration' from within. In this they were aided, in some cases, by the apprehension of an order in the universe transcending, and, to their minds, replacing, the unsatisfactoriness of the new industrial social setting; or, in others, by the realisation of possibilities of social organisation more satisfying than that which had, for them, lost all validity. But often a negative tendency was as marked as any positive effort towards reconstruction. Towards the end of the century, the art for art's sake movement found its *raison d'être* as much in the rejection of the bourgeois outlook as in its urge to find a valid basis for artistic creation. The desire *épater le bourgeois* provided much of the driving force behind a man like Oscar Wilde, for instance.

The social void naturally placed a much greater burden upon the individual; undisciplined by social conscience, finding in disobedience to what was contemptuously dismissed as bourgeois morality a mark of artistic validity, the writer became egotistical in the sense that George Santayana has given to the word:

It assumes, if it does not assert, that the source of one's being and power lies in oneself; that will and logic are by right omnipotent, and that nothing should control the mind or the conscience but itself.

And so the claims of society have been replaced by those of the individual, and right personal feeling has replaced right social behaviour. The morality of social intercourse, with its consequent restriction on the exploitations of 'personality' is replaced by the personal morality of the sensitive individual, who claims for his intuitions and perceptions a justification which may well bring him into conflict with what seem the coarser demands of society. In *Wuthering Heights*, the strength of the passion of Heathcliff and Cathy seems to provide its own justification; and from the time of the Brontës, at least, the genuineness of

personal experience rather than the verdict of an outworn social morality, has, for many, been the ultimate criterion.

Nevertheless, the position has always been felt to be unsatisfactory
and recently the need for some sort of re-integration, the necessity for
discovering on what grounds the intelligent individual can come to
terms with his social surroundings, has been more pressingly felt. It is
one of the problems of Mr E. M. Forster; and, if the marriage of a
Schlegel and a Wilcox in *Howard's End* is consciously felt as something
of a pious hope, the central conflict of the book depends on a realisation
that class and cultural antagonisms exist; and that behind class relationships lies the profounder problem of human relationships. This deeper
question has become immensely complicated in our age. There has
been, first, the relative absence of any traditional social standards by
which to judge individual behaviour. Then there has been an immense
increase in the possible ways of life offered by an old and incredibly
complicated civilisation. As a result of longevity, such fragments of
inherited conceptions, ideas, and perceptions as survive have, in a number of cases, become outworn; they have ceased to evolve in accordance
with the needs of the social realities of the day and retained power only
to clog and hinder a truer perception of social requirements, demanding
a correspondingly greater effort of individual integrity to cast them off.
Again, the boundaries of the individual personality have been so extended, as a result of the psychological discoveries of the last hundred
years, that what seemed before to be reasonably well-defined and know-
able has become uncertain and tentative—not by any means all loss, of
course, but tending to inhibit action and increase perplexity. As Mr
Forster points out: "Psychology has split and shattered the idea of a
'Person', and has shown that there is something incalculable in each
of us."

These problems of human relationships, of human self-consciousness, or, to use his own word, of 'self-hood', were, in their social and,
above all, cosmic settings, to exercise L. H. Myers in his five novels. He
first sought the naked personality behind the veils of illusion which men,
in their social life, spun around themselves. He wanted to know what
men were like without their masks. Then, when he had explored the
naked essence of social man, he sought a healthier basis for personal
relationship. There appears, as we follow his thought through, a progression towards a 'solution' in *The Pool of Vishnu* which, if it still
leaves the nature of the wider social integration a little shadowy and
obscure, nevertheless provides a possible approach to the problem of the
sensitive individual's feeling of isolation. If the success of a modern
artist (or of any artist) lies in his capacity to recreate sympathetically
and consistently the complexity of the individual problem in its personal

and social implications, the work of Myers must as a whole be judged successful.

The Orissers was his first novel, and appeared in 1922. It had been preceded by the publication, in 1908, of a play, *Arvat*. This, however, hardly warrants critical recognition. The emphasis in *The Orissers* is not so much on human relationships, as on the individual's predicament in a fleshy and material society which Myers cannot accept as an adequate milieu. The stress is on the individual's isolation in the inner recesses of his own ego, the burdens and illusions of selfhood. If the book is by no means entirely successful as a novel, for reasons which I shall try to explain later, it nevertheless exhibits the characteristic preoccupations of Myers in a somewhat raw and undigested state. A careful analysis of this first work will, therefore, be of assistance in pointing to the relative strengths and weaknesses that Myers exhibits in his novels; at the same time, it will lead us to the heart of Myers's problem.

The plot is comparatively simple; but as the book has been out of print for some time, it may be useful to recount it briefly. The novel resolves itself into a conflict, a contest which has spiritual implications, between the Orissers and the Maynes for the possession of the country estate, Eamor, which has belonged to the Orissers for five hundred years. After the death of her first husband, the distinguished archaeologist, Sir Charles Orisser, Lilian Orisser is forced to accept the financial aid of John Mayne, a wealthy business man, in straightening out her late husband's affairs. John Mayne has been a previous suitor, and, as a result of his intervention, it is tacitly assumed that Lilian will marry him; this she actually does. Husband and wife soon quarrel, however, and John Mayne banishes his wife to Eamor, where she lives with Nicholas, her step-son, a child of Charles Orisser by a previous marriage. She has another step-son, Cosmo, a step-brother of Nicholas; but Cosmo has turned renegade and is filled with a passionate hatred of Lilian. As a sign of her gratitude to John Mayne for his assistance, Lilian has taken out a heavy mortgage on the house of Eamor, which John Mayne accepts as a token payment. But Lilian is determined that when John Mayne dies, Eamor shall pass to herself and, later on, to Nicholas as the true heir of the Orissers. At Eamor she is eventually joined by Madeline Mayne, John Mayne's niece and later fiancée to Walter Standish, John Mayne's partner and successor to be. A deep enmity springs up between the two women, and Madeline desires to gain possession of Eamor, or at least to prevent her uncle from carrying out his verbal promise of handing the estate over to the Orissers. Even if she does not keep the estate herself, she wants the satisfaction of humiliating Lilian by handing over the mortgage to her. The presence of Cosmo in the neighbourhood is an added complication; he provides an alternative heir to whom John Mayne, if and when he learns of Cosmo's presence, could transfer Eamor, thus fulfilling his promise to keep Eamor in the Orisser family, and avenging himself, at the same time, on his wife.

Lilian, aided by Allen Allen, a former partner of her first husband, whose mistress she becomes and whom she finally marries, manages, in the end, to secure Eamor before the death of John Mayne, but not before Cosmo has been murdered by Allen and much intrigue has been necessary.

This however gives but a perfunctory account of the work; for as the central conflict is to be thought of in spiritual rather than material terms (so that Eamor is a symbol rather than a material possession) so the chief attraction of the novel lies in its examination of various possibilities of living. As a preface to the book, Myers printed an extract from Bacon's *Novum Organum:*

Four species of Illusions beset the human mind, to which (for distinction's sake) we have assigned names: calling the first, Illusions of the Tribe; the second, Illusions of the Den; the third, Illusions of the Market; the fourth, Illusions of the Schools.

.   .   .   .

The Illusions of the Tribe are inherent in human nature, and the very tribe or race of man. . . .

The Illusions of the Den are those of each individual. For everybody (in addition to the errors common to the race of man) has his own individual den or cavern, which intercepts and corrupts the light of nature. . . .

There are also Illusions formed by the reciprocal intercourse and society of man with man, which we call Illusions of the Market, from the commerce and association of men with each other. . . .

Lastly, there are Illusions which have crept into men's minds from the various dogmas of peculiar systems of philosophy. . . .

It is with these illusions in their various manifestations, especially as they affect the social life of man, that Myers is concerned. The Maynes and the Orissers are fundamentally opposed; their ways of life are incompatible and there is no possibility of a relationship which could bridge their spiritual divergence. As Allen expresses it: "Between John Mayne and us there is no spiritual connection."

The Maynes, with whom Walter Standish is also closely associated, represent, in their various ways, the worldly, material values of society. John Mayne is a financier whose spiritual obtuseness is reflected on the material level by the grossness of his bodily presence. To him his marriage is little more than the conclusion of a successful business deal; it involves only the desire for possession; worldly success and prestige provide the motive forces for this, as for all his other transactions. The marriage on these terms is a failure. There is a complete inability on the part of the two to make any form of spiritual contact. The rift is absolute; it is something beyond the conscious control of either party:

The deep volitions that lie at the unconscious depths of every human nature moved and shook the ground beneath their feet . . . Man's fundamental unity in aspiration was a myth; the simple old saying that one man's meat is another's poison was the first and last word in human philosophy.

This apprehension of fundamental antagonisms forms part of Myers's outlook at this time and makes his point of view self-consciously aristocratic in its implications. Thus Nicholas feels strongly a sense of isolation in the financial and commercial world of the Maynes, to whose standards of value the foulness of the industrial scene at Tornel, a neighbouring factory town, with its stunted denizens, provides a dreadful testimony:

But these men and women, they were his like, you would say? No, he denied it . . . he and his were their product evolved through many generations—their inferior, if you pleased—their parasite! But their like; no, only cant would maintain it.

And just as the incompatibility between the Maynes and the Orissers lies beyond conscious volition, so the attempt of John Mayne to gain a return in terms of love for the material goods which are all he has to offer is the sign of a deep-seated obtuseness which lies beyond the power of man to eradicate.

This conception of irremediable materialism lay at the root of Myers's views on society; and his spiritual fastidiousness condemned the self-glorification of a social order that can see

no excellence excepting in service to itself, and gradually, but infallibly loses sight of all but material values. It consequently exacts terrible renunciation from its members—the deadliest and easiest being the suppression of a sense of renunciation.

This problem, characteristically translated into abstract terms, is, of course, indicative of the difficulties which have exercised the sensitive for the last century. They confronted Henry James. In Tolstoi they provided a motive for social action. The world of Babbitt, with its gross moral values, its spiritual obtuseness, its grasping after the tangible and the assessable, its Philistinism, has explicitly concerned the artist since the time of Matthew Arnold. There are more than hints of the problem in Wordsworth and Shelley, where the spiritual malaise inseparable from the romantic view of life already takes on a sharpened social awareness. Wordsworth was conscious of the corroding influence of the busy world of men; Tintern Abbey plays for him a part recognisably related to, though more concretely graspable than, that which Eamor plays for the Orissers, and, by implication, for Myers.

Myers stresses the ethical side of the problem, for he is more concerned with ethics and conduct than with what are termed cultural values; 'sweetness and light', as interpreted by the later nineteenth century and many of the artists of Myers's own day, was too liable to degenerate into a petty aestheticism and thus did not gain his approval. It is 'character', not in the public school sense of that over-worked word but in its deeper implications of living in consonance with man's most profound intuitions, which exercises Myers's mind. So much is this so that a full account of his analysis of the materialist outlook will do much to take us to what he conceives to be the central problem of living.

It is of the essence of the materialist spirit, according to Myers, that its ultimate appeal is to public opinion; it is evoked by too great an attention to what the world thinks, and accepts as the ultimate touchstones of blamelessness, public opinion, and common law. It fosters those illusions of the Market which blind men to the truer guidance of the inner spirit; it accepts social, rather than spiritual, criteria.

In most of Myers's books there is a group of characters who represent what he called 'the world'. By the 'world' he meant society as it manifested itself in the life of social classes and institutions. In society standards of conduct were derived, ultimately, not from an apprehension of spiritual forces comprehending something greater than, and apart from, man, but from a glorification of society's own spirit, a judgement in terms of its own materialistic values. Most people, he considered, lived by appearances; by 'appearances' he usually implied those modes of behaviour, those masks, which a man adopts so that he may find himself accepted. Such a man presents to his companions a recognisable 'personality', a 'persona'. Myers, in fact, belongs to that group of romantic writers who exploit the sort of situation inherent in Rousseau, who posit a cleavage between the 'real' man and the social man and who seek to uncover the genuine traits of personality beneath all the accretions which society imposes. One feels Myers's criticisms to be valid because in complex societies like our own, such artificialities do, in fact, exist in the terms in which he describes them; and his analysis of them, his appreciation of certain types of twentieth-century self-consciousness and of certain restrictions in self-knowledge that society encourages, are acute and perceptive. Moreover, the dichotomy of man and society in his novels is more acutely realised than is often the case in such analyses. He sees that the acceptance of such conventional and inadequate conduct is not the inevitable response to social conditions: man

is a free being, and has the capacity for choice and discrimination. Not
all submit to the prevarications of society; and it is possible to conceive
a more valid form of social relationship where such temptations as the
'world' provides will be obviated. The essence of the situation is described at the beginning of *The Near and the Far*; Hari and Jali are talking
together:

"I think life frightens you?" said Hari, smiling. Jali coloured and still remained
silent.
"Not to be afraid of this world," said Hari slowly, "you must belong to it."
"Ah, but how?" thought Jali.
"One can always pretend to oneself that one does," Hari went on, looking at
him intently. "Didn't I tell you once that in a nightmare the way to escape from
a pursuing tiger is to turn oneself into one?"
"Yes."
"Pretend to yourself that you are like others," said Hari carelessly. "Everyone
is doing it."
"But if everyone is pretending to be like others, who is like himself?"

The final question is very pertinent to the whole investigation. For, by
pretending to be like others, one lives up to a preconceived, but fundamentally illusory, standard of conduct:

by calling for certain appearances, you expressed yourself as a type, you exhibited certain recognised features, a stock personality; you gave people a plain,
straightforward reading of your character.

Such behaviour involves illusion because it invokes a standard which
values only the arid social *conventions* of the day; it represses the spontaneous self of the individual, the uniqueness of personality, and prevents one from entering freely and spontaneously into relationship with
other human beings. It represents Myers's version of Mr E. M. Forster's
'undeveloped heart'.

In John Mayne the wordly spirit manifests itself in a desire for a
success which will bring public and open approbation. His relationship
with Lilian, as we have seen, involves little more than a cash deal; but
his marriage provides only one manifestation of a way of life which has
produced an inner paralysis because it has depended for its justification
on the social gesture, the charitable bequest, the life of 'service' with
the nuance that the world commonly gives the word. Even his preliminary tenderness to Lilian at the beginning of their married life is
corrupted by a sense of achievement, a desire to show her off as a trophy
to his friends to leer at; this produces in Lilian a physical, as well as a
spiritual, revulsion: "as though [his friends] actually held her between
finger and thumb."
Condemnation of this mode of conduct is contained in a vision which

Nicholas has of a *tête-à-tête* between himself and John Mayne. In this dream, Mayne's fault is revealed as a falsification of the scriptural injunction: "Let not your right hand know what your left hand doeth." Mayne is supposed to say: "I have followed the precept and found it good. Whilst busily using one hand to encompass the good of others, I have let the other work instinctively, unconsciously, to my own advantage." His conduct, indeed, has produced a lack of inner coherence; he has become a two-headed Janus of harshness and brutality on the one side and sentimental idealism on the other. The lack of self-questioning, of inner searching, the unwillingness to bring into play the deeper faculties of the soul, the readiness to surrender to a 'free emotionalism' give men of the John Mayne type their vitality, their ability to face and conquer the world because they are of the world, and because they accept its values. They are like the Wilcoxes in *Howard's End*—they do not 'connect'. Indeed, though the analysis has differences of stress, Forster's words on the Wilcoxes of the world have their relevance here:

> Pierpoint Morgan has never said 'I' in his life. No superman can say 'I want' because 'I want' must lead to the question 'who am I'? and so to Pity and Justice. He only says 'want'—'Want Europe' if he's Napoleon; 'want wives' if he's Bluebeard; 'want Botticelli' if he's Pierpoint Morgan. Never 'I' and if you could pierce through him, you'd find panic and emptiness in the middle.

In his false idealism, his sentimental benevolences, Mayne bears a close resemblance, too, to D. H. Lawrence's Thomas Crich; in his surrender of personal relationships to 'material interests' he owes something to Conrad's Charles Gould. When John Mayne comes up against the more sensitive awareness of the Orissers he comes to a realisation of what can be described at least as inadequacy. The 'I' has not been fully developed; the personality, despite its ability to impose itself on the worldly, is embryonic—his relationship to others remains that of the world of 'it' rather than of 'thou', to use Martin Buber's phraseology. He is even capable of relishing "insincerity as a tribute to power"—only the Orissers can pierce the public character and keep him, half reluctant, to a sense of moral obligation.

And yet, John Mayne is at least the honest enemy; there is in him an element of self-awareness, even if that awareness emerges only after the dissolution of the hard crust of 'personality' through acid contact with the Orissers. Mayne's business associate, Walter Standish, is the dishonest enemy. He stands as the perfect prototype of the public figure; he lacks even the individual vitality, the coarser manifestations of exuberant nature, which give John Mayne's character, at its worst, a certain personal validity. As with Peer Gynt, so with Standish; once

the layers of the onion have been removed, there is no core or centre
left. His being is a façade, a series of elaborately learnt social gestures;
his morality is one which has been picked up on the road to worldly
success; his liberalism—and he is a man of 'liberal culture'—is that of
a new school, of those "who only rode the chariot of reform in order
surreptitiously to apply the brake." If John Mayne was capable of taking
up a certain cynical detachment in thinking of his own charitable
bequests, Walter was unable to see his own conduct in any light but
that of public opinion. He has the awful sincerity of complete unawareness; he is the 'good' man in all his moral obtuseness, the public
'idealist' in all his impenetrability. There is no possibility of any response to a particular situation, of an inner re-ordering; all is external-
ised, devitalised:

He liked to transcribe every particular problem into general terms, and then
treat it according to the rules laid down for the man of probity, who is also a
man of the world.

Anything which is unpleasant, which does not fit in with an idealised
conception of human affairs, like Allen's revelation that Lilian is his
mistress, is dismissed. To admit such things would be to recognise a
depth in human affairs, a possibility of dark subterranean forces which
would militate against his idealism, an idealism which merely consists
of the social conformities invested with a spurious high-mindedness:

For all his man-of-the-worldishness, Walter remains very ingenuous at heart,
and sexual misconduct inspires him with a particular horror which he is ashamed
to confess.

Even his love for Madeline is the result of careful fore-thought and
prudence; for like calls to like, and despite her sexuality, which is
merely the sexuality of overt display, sex socialised, as it were, he realises that she will make no demand on him for "expenditures" of passion
greater than "can be comfortably afforded." The metaphor drawn
from the world of monetary transactions correctly places the relationship. And so he maintains those ignorances which are the "pre-requisite
of his own blamelessness"—those

proud, simple-minded ignorances which were the very substructure of his
honour and self-respect.

His friend, Harry Portman, that very capable civil servant, who makes
a brief, impersonal appearance in the novel, provides him with his
standard; he, too, accepts social opinion and legal standards of right-
eousness. Inaction is Standish's method of dealing with the pressing
problems of human relationships. Wholly incapable of any passionate

feeling of any sort, he is Mr Facing-Both-Ways in his desire for detachment and fairness of mind and his insistence on a sense of proportion
except where worldly ends and values are at stake:

The young man [Nicholas] recognised beneath Walter's phrases a spirit of
good intention, a quality that came so near to sincerity that one could not
properly ignore it. But was Walter's belief in his own sincerity justified? Was
Walter really and truly prepared to plunge to the very heart of the problem?
. . . In how puzzled a manner would Walter knit his brows! How kindly he
would try to understand, and how satisfactorily he would fail! How urbanely
he would evade. . . . And he foresaw only too well how all these manoeuvres
—that glassy look of defensive non-comprehension in particular—would
madden him.

Walter illustrates, as Allen says, the "average written large"; he is a
living representative of the copy-book maxims, a walking embodiment
of those virtues which society endorses, and which he combines with
the anaemic and complacent Puritanical merits of self-help and prudence. He is a perpetual cliché among human types. His epitaph may
be taken from the preface to Shelley's *Alastor*; he is one of those "meaner
spirits" who,

deluded by no generous error, instigated by no sacred thirst of doubtful knowledge, duped by no illustrious superstition, loving nothing on this earth and
cherishing no hopes beyond, yet aloof from sympathies with their kind, re-
joicing neither in human joy nor mourning with human grief.

For he belongs to the "unforeseeing multitudes" of the "morally
dead," and his great moment is a moment of almost perfect dishonesty,
a supreme and final opportunity for avoiding any genuine moral issue,
of having to face with any degree of inner probity an ethical problem.
    But if Walter is Public Virtue embodied (and the nature of Myers's
social criticism of the world of public relationships can be guessed at
from the underlying irony which accompanies so many of Walter's
musings), Madeline, though of a more exuberant personality, and less
successful and therefore more avid in her idealisation of life, provides
the perfect consort. The analysis of Madeline is one of the most successful features of the book. For the roots of Madeline's composition spring
from an over-emotionalism which is dissatisfied with any relationship
which is not a tribute to her power to exploit the feelings of others, and
from which, while seeming to give, she would be able to absorb more
than she presented. For she is unable to conceive of intercourse as between equals; she must dominate. She stands for that particular type of
emotionally exuberant woman who finds, in an 'idealised' but falsified
service to others, some consolation for a deep, inner impoverishment.
What she would seem to offer is herself; what more subtly she would

gain is power over the lives of others. Affection, devotion involve not the freely exchanged intercourse of equals but provide the means of securing vantage. She is the Managing Female, who cannot meet life on adult terms but whose capacity for emotional blackmail is the spiritual counterpart of John Mayne's pecuniary triumphs, the object of both being power—"the power to guide, direct and control the destiny of those with whom" they come into contact. She can only feel herself truly alive before an audience; for, lacking that capacity which Pascal found to be the mark of the truly free spirit, of resting alone with her own soul for a quarter of an hour, she finds her identity only in the imposition of her personality on others:

Unless she could manifest herself in voice and gesture before an appreciative audience and thus obtain material confirmation of what she believed herself to feel and think, she lost her sense of being truly alive, she became oppressed by a sentiment of personal nullity.

To know about the affairs of others was to give her that sense of superiority which was necessary for her well-being. Fed on the petty confederacies, the small disreputable intimacies of her own home, she naturally feels that the circle of the Orissers will present her with similar opportunities for emotional intercourse and domination. Her reaction to the aloofness and coldness of Nicholas, Isabel, and Lilian is a hatred which is her supreme condemnation. Her appeal, as we have seen, is to a public; and at Eamor there was "no appeal to public judgement." She mistakes appearance for reality; and her dictum "we must idealise or we should cease to struggle" is a mark of her need to invest the ordinary unsatisfactory realities of every-day life with a spurious transcendentalism. A willingness to see things as they really are appears to her a manifestation of an unhuman cynicism; and her hatred for Lilian, especially, springs from a fundamental discrepancy between her underlying mental expectations which have been disappointed and her idealisation which has been outraged by Lilian's mode of life. Hence, the constant scenes between the two; and hence the momentary exhaustion of Madeline's pent-up emotional forces, inducing in its turn a renewed desire for contact, a desire which finds its expression in a peculiarly nauseating form of pseudo-Christian forgiveness. Reconciliation only provides an opportunity for another type of display springing from her ever abundant emotional vitality; it betrays a need for a debased form of spiritual refreshment, so that the temporarily exhausted resources of her false idealism can receive replenishment from conduct as corrupt in its positive as in its negative manifestations. A similar situation arises in the relationship between Baron de Mauves and his wife in Henry James's story, *Madame de Mauves*: "Longmore

fancied that the Baron was more irritated than gratified by his wife's
irreproachable reserve. Did it dimly occur to him that it was self-control
and not self-effacement? She was a model of all the inferior matrons of
his line, past and to come, and an occasional 'scene' from her at a convenient moment would have something reassuring—would attest her
stupidity a trifle more forcibly than her inscrutable tranquillity."

And so, Madeline, with all her formidability, provides only another
manifestation of the world. Yet, as with John Mayne, strength and
tenacity are on her side. For Myers is acutely conscious that vitality and
exuberance lie in general with those who draw their strength from the
world, who are conscious of majority support, who flow with the
coarse, vulgar tide of living symbolised in the novel by Tornel, Harry
Portman and that world of "huge hotels" where "each bulky guest
represented something equally bulky in the realm of finance." The
lack of intellectual and moral effort implied by such a way of life gives
a vitality which needs to be expressed in purely mundane ways. Those
who have never renounced (or, to put it another way, are unaware that
they have ever renounced, which amounts to the same thing) can draw
from the life of society an instinctive self-justification which, because it
is supported by all they see about them, provides no discipline and calls
for no voluntary self-realisation in anything outside society. Indeed,
occasional half-conscious perception of other values only evokes a more
frenzied seeking after the public virtues; for to the conscious search for
approbation is added the additional emotional drive of an unconscious
fear. Such a fear leads to Madeline's loss of control in her scene with
Lilian over Nicholas's seduction of his young cousin, Isabel. It is the
unconscious element in the relationship between the two women that
upsets Madeline's carefully laid plans and makes her take refuge in a
display of temper she is unable to check.

The Maynes, then, stand for 'life'—life as a matter of emotion and
domination, life that

dotes on variety, with plenty of movement, plenty of scope for the emotions,
plenty of what is commonly called 'action' and 'character'. And its purpose to
distract us from the real conflict, to be sure!—the conflict that no one talks
about, if he can help it—the conflict between life on the one side, and on the
other, Boredom, Disgust, and Fear.

So John Mayne, in Nicholas's vision, sums it up—and that, perhaps, is
how a more self-aware John Mayne would have expressed it. Their
contact with 'life' in this superficial sense, is stressed in Myers's descriptions of their physical make-up. John Mayne is a huge coarse organism:
and, looking at Walter and Madeline together, on the way for a horse
ride, Mayne notes with pleasure how they stand

as delineators of corporeal vigour and nothing more. In them, he saw, albeit unwittingly, an expression of life's willingness to dispense with spiritual significance. . . . He saw in the haunches of horses, in their nostrils, in the throat and bosom of the girl, in her hips, in her lips, in every line and feature of those carnally resplendent bodies, nothing but a brutal exposition of the self-sufficingness of the flesh.

And yet, as has already been hinted, all these manifestations of life, all these expressions of an apparently unselfconscious vitality, are at bottom subject to an inward dissatisfaction. For, despite the approbation of the world, there remains an inner void; there is an emptiness which, when public approval is no longer there, when the test of contact with personalities deeper in their spiritual awareness is undergone, becomes evident. As in *The Root and the Flower*,

contact with Amar's mind . . . had the effect of concentrating Hari's attention upon the 'vulgarity' of Daniyal. His sense of it in the past had remained floating in suspension; a drop of acid from Amar's particular fastidiousness had been needed to precipitate it,

so their relationship with the Orissers forces upon the Maynes an intuition of the inadequacy of their own way of life. Myers was aware of those subterranean channels of communication, of those intuitive apprehensions which lie below the manifestation of the conscious life and which play so large a part in our communings one with another. Madeline's scenes with Lilian, Walter's indignant repudiation of Allen's disclosures, are tributes to the Orissers, indications of their superior mode of life which acts as a constant challenge to the coarser standards of the Maynes. And John Mayne, at least, half recognises this. His attempts to play Lilian's 'game' as he calls it, fail; but in the process,

he began to lose that quality which is the saving grace of such men, their spiritual obtuseness.

A subtle self-hate begins to seize him; Eamor becomes an obsession. The mere existence of the Orissers acts as a challenge, provokes a probing criticism which undermines his self-confidence. The Orissers triumph over him merely because they occupy a place in his consciousness. And yet they stand for "what life [in John Mayne's sense of the word] intended should be ignored."

In a sense, the Orissers do stand for "Boredom, Disgust, and Fear"; self-awareness, the exercise of the critical spirit, ability and sincerity, a capacity to stand outside the self, are conceived by Myers as involving, in a subtle way, a rejection of the normal processes of vulgar living. The problem of the Orissers is the problem of the sensitive which arose at the time of the Renaissance and which the Romantic writers later made their own. Their spirit is the protestant spirit. The burden of the mystery lies on the self and ultimately the self cannot bear the burden. It is a phase of the Hamlet problem, the sensitive, self-critical mind which can accept nothing—"that would be scann'd." Such a mind can make no real contact with the external world because what it finds there, whether it be the "spirit of competition" that "so largely insulates man from man," the necessary hypocrisies of public life where men conspire together to forget the realities, or the uncanalised sexuality which permeates the new materialism and which needs to disguise itself under a false idealism[1]—the scheme, as Nicholas says "to invest society with all the dignity and authority of religion,"—is unacceptable. Hamlet bears with him the 'Embassy of Death'; he stands outside life, because any manifestation of the critical spirit, any ability to abstract oneself from the flow of existence, in order to see the Self or part of the Self as separate identity, involves a removal from immediate living, an appreciation of the essential gap between desire and fulfilment.

Something of this lies at the root of the problem of the Orissers. There is some reason in John Mayne's condemnation of Nicholas, as there is in Hamlet's self-condemnation:

for you and your like life is nothing but death-in-life. You are the small and sickly child, against which Mother Nature turns in disgust! She persecutes it, because it is moved to traduce her. You are life's antipathy! You are one of those who radiate darkness and disease! Where you go a blight runs before you; colours fade; sounds are deadened; the earth is corroded; the sky tarnished; and the chill of sickness is communicated to living, human hearts!

But if "living, human hearts" means Claudius and Gertrude, or the Maynes, it is preferable to accept Boredom, Disgust, and Fear rather than the inner corruptions and evasions of the living; for those who, like Macbeth, lose the "taste of fears" may yet lose other more vital sources of personality. And if the life of society, as seen by a clear and uncorrupted vision, has nothing to offer it is as well to accept the fact. The position is not satisfactory, perhaps. The Orrisers are aware of their aridity; they are cold, and, not only to Madeline, "depressingly empty of idealism, painfully deficient in aspiration"; they lack heart and vitality. Lilian herself admits the need for new blood in their veins. They exist on the higher cerebral levels and the blight of self-consciousness has fallen on each. They feel like Stephen Dedalus:

To merge his life in the common tide of other lives was harder for him than any fasting or prayer, and it was his constant failure to do this to his own satisfaction which caused in his soul at last a sensation of spiritual dryness together with a growth of doubts and scruples;

[1] Cf. D. H. Lawrence's remarks, in *Fantasia* and elsewhere, on the relationship between 'idealism' and 'materialism'.

or like Thomas Mann's Tonio Kröger, who senses the position of the
artist as 'extra-human'—"For sound natural feeling, say what you
like, has no taste." Unlike Tonio Kröger, however, Nicholas realises
that there is no comfortable middle class which he can envy, no "bliss
of the commonplace" or "familiar minor happiness" that he can seek.
But just as Tonio reveals that the artist's gifts rest upon extremely sinister foundations, so Myers hints at criminal depths in at least one of his
Orissers, and associates the others, with remarkable nonchalance, in
murder, adultery, and a sort of experimental fornication. They consti-
tute Myers's version of the 'criminal artist'. Consciously or unconsciously, he allows them to partake of something of the spirit of Raskolnikov.
The exploration of their isolation takes its place among a vast number
of similar investigations within that decaying moral order which, for
so many writers, constitutes the modern world.

Cosmo is the one most critically aware of the world. As a creation
he is not wholly satisfactory, for Myers does not seem to have conveyed
the character in all its possible implications. Though a wastrel in his
early life, Cosmo has followed his Vision; for, as he writes:

This world is a caricature, a changeling, substituted by some ugly trick. We
are not in the Real World;

but in one that reveals its true reality only in flashes. His sincerity is
continually stressed:

The article called truth, and commonly exchanged as such in the commerce of
life—the article that most persons consider good enough to offer to themselves
and to others—that article, compared with the stuff that Cosmo dealt in, was
shoddy.

As a result of this his spirit is continually in revolt against Actuality—
the Ideal (in the visionary, not in the social sense of the Maynes) is
present before his eyes as a direct Intuition. It does not matter that this
vision is unrealisable; it stands over against the shoddy materialism of
the new society of Maynes and Standishes, and it is a vision to be preserved. Yet his insight is that of a madman. He demands too much, and
his malignancy at disappointment is continually stressed. This appears
to arouse in him a "self-conscious, critical, and consequently Satanic
spirit," or so at least Allen expresses it. Here, of course, is something
of the Satanism of the Romantic Agony. He was born into the world
with visions of perfection "and our humanity was necessarily a defile-
ment to him,"—so Nicholas analyses him. He brought with him a
knowledge of Paradise and the actuality of humanity can only appear
a sorry and shoddy replica. But in the end humanity has dragged him
down—his body has betrayed him. For to enter this world is to accept

Good and Evil; and so it would appear that the satanic spirit has developed and he who has soared to Heaven now grovels in Hell. The
vision has faded; there remains only a profound sincerity, a sincerity
which can strip all those ignorances so vital to our mental health and
which is yet daemonic because it reveals the subterranean "evil things
in robes of snow" which stand over against life as the world knows it.
Cosmo probes the foul depths of sinful humanity; no Freudian censor,
no "zealous porter at the doors of the consciousness" prevents him
from revealing what he finds. This porter is "the man Cosmo has assassinated." His revelation of the psychic depths convinces Allen that the
"social ideals of a utilitarian age [are] totally inadequate to satisfy the unconscious energies of mankind." The ultimate truth of things provoked
by Cosmo's self-awareness seems, in fact, to involve an appreciation of
the miseries of the world that "are misery and will not let [one] rest."[1]
Myers, in so far as he sympathises with Cosmo, faces the possibility
of Nihilism, the negation of life in all its aspects which is, paradoxically,
what Cosmo's vision has turned into—too great light has blinded. It is
this, perhaps, that justifies Allen's murder of Cosmo, so that at least
Eamor may be preserved; while he lives Cosmo proves an alternative
heir through whom John Mayne can fulfil his promise. It is the appreciation of the love of Allen and Lilian, the realisation that there are in
fact positive values in normal, actual life which leads Nicholas to reject
Cosmo, and which in a vision he has of Cosmo on a theatre stage, makes
him shrink with horror from the performance.

Yet Nicholas, like Cosmo at the end of his life when his idealism had
become nihilistic, also lives, as Allen diagnoses, on the higher cerebral
levels. Allen, if anyone, represents the man of decent human achievement and action in the novel; he at least has come to terms with life, as
Nicholas states, at the price of a certain mental inertia. Allen demonstrates to Nicholas certain inadequacies in the latter's way of life; by
continual self-questionings, by constant intellectual penetration (and
Myers was already developing something of an anti-intellectual bias)
Nicholas has arrived at a position which divides the spirit and the flesh
into two self-contained units. His seduction of Isobel is pure egotism,
and he analyses, coldly and self-consciously, the progress of the affair
and its inevitable waning. For, to him, love is Venus, not Isis, mother
of life; it springs from the desire to find self-expression in another
rather than from an urge towards creation and relationship. Despite his
wish to use his inwardness as a means of creation, Nicholas remains
sterile. He has the characteristics of the sceptic and he shows many of
the unsatisfactory qualities to which scepticism leads. He is described
as having a "face expressive of melancholy which would easily turn

[1] Cf. Keats, *The Fall of Hyperion*. (The revised *Hyperion*.)

to scorn"—a scorn which, as a mode of self-protection, he frequently directs against others. He can gain nothing from his affair with Isobel because his sceptical mind has already fixed the progress of the experience in advance, and hence destroyed it before it has begun to live. He has left nothing to creation, to instinct, which belongs, as Allen says, to the organic life, and might well have helped to transcend the intellectually pre-ordained experience, offering a change into something new. There is none of that coalescence between subject and object which Coleridge sensed as the pre-requisite to creative life, no 'I-thou' relationship. Hence the deadness, the aridity of the life of those Orissers who commune only on the higher intellectual levels and for whom existence becomes, as in Lilian, the mere performance of a number of pre-ordained functions. Aware constantly as he is of his own inadequacy Nicholas realises that his interest is in ideas rather than people; yet his analysis of Madeline and Walter obviously has Myers's approval. With Nicholas's self-consciousness goes a sense of difference that is made explicit in his contrasting of himself with the people of Tornel: "Their inferior, if you pleased—their parasite! But their like; no, only cant would maintain it." This sense of isolation, reflected in the physical remoteness of Eamor, has a double significance for Myers. In so far as Nicholas stands over against the Walters and the Madelines, Myers approves; yet John Mayne's criticism, already quoted, obviously has some force. Nicholas is one of the finer spirits of the drama; but his internal conflict, though a mark of spiritual awareness, is, nevertheless, not to be conceived of as representing a positive standard. Myers is too aware of the Satanic element in critical self-consciousness, not to express uneasiness at the nihilism of a Cosmo or the failure at integration of a Nicholas. The condemnation of the intellect was to play an important part in his thought, as we shall see. In Nicholas, the counterpart on a more cerebral level of those romantic failures that strew the pages of modern literature after the fashion of romanticised Hamlets, Myers explores the illusions of the Schools and, perhaps, of the Den. Nicholas was a character with whom Myers took especial pains; he realised that Nicholas represented something in himself; as Mrs Myers has told me: "he loved Nicholas." Nicholas is aware of his own aridity and failure; for him the paradox of living consists of the fact that,

To be alive is to offer resistance to the flux, to contract out of the general fluidity into a hard discreetness, to curdle into independent self-consciousness. And yet it is true that self-consciousness turns living into a mummery.

And if the answer is that he has too small a heart, his further reply is:

What's the heart of a man, that has no counterpart in the universe, no ensample in the mind of a God?

To those unable to come to terms with the universe or with a God, the problem is insoluble; the only refuge lies in the separation of the emotional and the intellectual sides of man's nature. Hence Isobel is to Nicholas ultimately a thing and Lilian only a communicating intelligence. From none of his experiences can he develop emotionally, because that part of his nature which can learn cannot enter into, coalesce with, his experience: ". . . deep in his heart was the sense that the lure of the external, the extraneous, was vulgar and elusive. All true wealth was elaborated within." And so he is left alone with his selfhood, and all his life is but a progress towards spiritual death. He cannot marry Isobel; he cannot enter the world; for to find a mystical value in mere living is to him but a means by which humanity saves its own face. Concentration, the development of the intrinsic, is his ideal, a cultivation of arid Being without the necessity of a vain issue in Becoming. Externals have just sufficient claim on him to lead him to renounce Cosmo; for he is not, like Cosmo, completely lost to life—with Lilian at least he can commune, if only on a cerebral level. Yet obsessed by the burden of Selfhood, he can accept none of the conventional methods of release. The Ego will always remain, "the unalterable substrate for ever be present." He stands between the two worlds, one dead, the other powerless to be born.

His predicament, then, is that of the modern intellectual involved in the romantic dilemma, of the mind that has turned in upon itself, that can find in no experience as such an adequate release from the consciousness of self. On the one side of him is Isobel, who seems to be deficient in any instinct of self-preservation at all and who is, in any case, but a shadowy figure in the novel; on the other, Lilian, misused by contact with John Mayne, who has learnt the value of a weary grace, of a sweet, enervating indolence. More acutely aware of those who surround her than is Nicholas, she seeks salvation in self-control, though her comment is: "how tiring." She possesses, in the higher reaches of her mental being, "some undiscovered chamber of her mind—or of the heart—to which she could repair." And this spirituality, which acts merely by its existence as a subconscious criticism of Madeline's demand for the display of a vulgar emotionalism, expresses itself in an apparent coldness; she achieves nevertheless a discipline of self which, if it allows vulgar life to pass by, will yet achieve some sort of beauty. That such a self-dedication, that the self-conscious creation of such an effect, is empty and sterile she is prepared to admit; but in a world that is constituted as the Maynes have made it, an elegant ritual within the walls and under the spiritual influence of Eamor is the best that can be achieved. Even her casting off of restraint in response to Allen is only a temporary affair. Like Nicholas, she is too abstracted from experience to integrate

herself adequately into any new social existence. Her life involves too
much a sort of self-perpetuating ritual which, if it acquires serenity, is,
in a way different from that of Nicholas but with similar results, fundamentally arid. Her marriage with Allen, though happy, is nevertheless
inadequate; for she has attained a self-sufficiency which goes even
further than his:

He needed the world of time and matter as stuff from which to distil the
abstraction of his thought. She, like an Indian Yogi, was learning to need
nothing.

And so, in the "dreadful peace of Eamor" she and Nicholas lead their
disenchanted lives, both divorced from life in its cruder manifestations;
Lilian, representative of a social disintegration, an embodiment of
gestures that have lost their significance, and Nicholas, victim of his
own intellectualism, spirits that "communicate without uniting," as
the flesh "unites without communicating."

Allen Allen, one time partner of Sir Charles Orisser, Lilian's first
husband, is the only member of the Orisser group whose life manages
to maintain something of a balance between the demands of mind and
matter. Whereas for Nicholas the two are necessarily divided, Allen
is early made aware of the insistent power of the material; for, as he
sits musing on the roof of a house in Tornel, after assenting to travel
with Cosmo, seemingly "raised above the small coercions of life," his
attention is attracted by a small persistent noise, the hiss of a steam jet
from a factory nearby:

That busy, unremitting sound was beginning to oppress him. It even
affected him with apprehension. That was the voice of matter—a reminder
of the wear and tear of quotidian things, and of the abject condition of
earthliness. That was what went on and on and beat you in the end.

Allen is an adventurer to whom life is a game of chance. An interest
in archaeology brings him into contact with Sir Charles Orisser. Unlike that of Sir Charles, however, his concern has relevance to the
contemporary world. His discovery of the past is really a means towards
integration, and such discovery, not abstract learning, is his aim: "He
believed that his subject matter might be made to reveal the subconscious intuitions and desires of all mankind." Fascinated by the mystery
of Time, he does not share Sir Charles's indifference to the present, but,
"by a healthy turn of mind," (the word 'healthy' is significant) summons to his aid the present. If, as he exclaims to Nicholas, "I couldn't
find in Thebes what I value in Tornel, I would let the past go hang;"
and Sir Charles's indifference to his present-day surroundings seems to
him reprehensible.

For Allen, then, the past is significant, not as an escape from, but as an enrichment of, the present. For him it is a *point d'appui*; if to Nicholas the gods in black basalt of the museum are pleasant because of their detachment from contemporaneity, expecting no worship, for Allen,

"in the graven images of Thoth and Ptah, of Seb and Set, other demiurges of the world stood present . . . [He continues:] And I felt that in my beating heart and in my flowing blood, and in the people of the city outside, and in all the life of the earth, those same energies were moving, august and resistless."

He is aware, that is to say, of continuity, of a community of human life on a cosmic scale. In his condemnation of Nicholas he regrets the dualism that has arisen "between the animal life of the race and the volition of the individual" and the loss of that immediate unity, of that organic relationship with the life of mankind which the critical self-consciousness of the individual has introduced. What are needed at the present day, he considers, are

larger personalities, in which the individual elements of mind, such as reason and will, shall be harmonised with the deeper instincts of race, to form one living whole.

The conscious values of the intellect are shifting, artificial—as

filii terrae we live by our instinctive, and largely unconscious, values, which are the values of the Great Mother.

This informs his reply to the critical nihilism of Cosmo, once the latter has lost his vision of possible life; this lies behind his justification for the murder of his erstwhile friend. For Cosmo would attack Eamor, which at least has its roots in some sort of tradition, cut off from healthy life though it may be. And the daring execution of his plan of attack against Cosmo and his interview with Walter on the train to Eamor when he discloses his relationship with Lilian reveal a mind that has correctly assessed the type of being it has to deal with. For (as Nicholas admits) Allen has sensibility and imagination. And, as has been re-marked, it is his realisation that Lilian is justified in her love for Allen that makes Nicholas abandon his friendship for Cosmo. And yet even Allen fails in his human relationship with Lilian; for fundamentally he is not dependent on it. All Allen really needs is his work; his conscious-ness of his absorption in the life of humanity as a whole has the effect of making the individual of lesser importance.

What then emerges from this study—and study it is rather than novel—of these different human types? Certain important features of Myers's outlook can be disentangled.

There is, of course, his constant concern for the essential character in persons, his continual investigation into the nature and springs of conduct. Although he restricts himself to a limited social milieu, that of the rich and leisured, in this and other novels, his characters reach beyond the class of society to which they belong. Thus in the condemnation of the parasitical and the emotionally uneducated we are made to feel, not that these are members of a particular class, but that they represent more permanent impulses of meanness and triviality which are reproduced at all social levels; and, by contrast, that the situation of those who are spiritually aware is not that of a small and elegant group, but raises problems which are valid for all who are concerned with the dignity of man, and the moral worth of human existence.

Myers realises the power of money; from this springs his condemnation of the material spirit of present-day society, his repudiation of that self-glorification in the communities of men which is a mark of the new materialism. Of this materialism the intellectual counterpart is Humanism, a creed, as Allen says, "which will only appeal to moral eunuchs"; an apt name, as Nicholas expresses it, "for a religion as proper to despiritualised man as Apianism to bees and Porcinism to pigs." To oppose the dismal life of mutual social back-scratching which is a product of the Maynes and Standishes, and which is merely a system of vicarious hedonism, it is necessary to conceive spiritual ends and to achieve some sort of integration in the life of the race. This is a vital element in Myers's thought and he returns to it over and over again—in Allen, in Wentworth of *Strange Glory*, in the Guru and in Gokal in *The Near and the Far*. Human relationships are not always enough; man must by mystical intuition set himself to rights with the universe. As Wentworth expresses it in *Strange Glory*:

I live here (in the forest) not in order to be alone, but to feel connected. . . . That feeling comes up, I think, from the earth. We all have our feet upon a common earth, our bodies are all built out of a common mould, we all spring from similar ancestors . . . : it is in the feel of the earth that we get the feel of humanity.

The urge towards redressing social irregularities, the performance of good works of a social nature are, as Myers sees, too often the result of an inner frustration and disappointment. The inner life is contrasted with the emptiness of a social existence which can only see its *raison d'être* in the approval of others. This provides the basis for Myers's belief that conventional morality is not a safe guide to conduct. Murder and adultery are excused in Myers's eyes by the sanction of the higher worth of the Orissers, and because Eamor is necessary to them for a continuance of their way of life. This represents Myers's version of that condemnation of bourgeois morality which is so common among romantic writers. There is a latent aristocratism in his tempered approval of the Orissers. All men, he believes, are subject to illusions based on the incorrect apprehension of things; yet some notions of conduct are more worth preserving than others. He condemns the false idealism of the Maynes as investing the reality of things with the values of society. "The character [an outward crust, or public confession of what the individual is like] develops at the expense of the perceptions and the imagination." Truth to self may, in a society which so inhibits genuine relationship, lead to aridity; but this is preferable to a spurious sociality.

There emerges, too, his awareness of the inadequacy of the intellect's capacity for creation. At the same time he is aware of the power of intuitive methods of communication; the effect of Lilian on John Mayne and Nicholas's apprehension at Allen's meeting with Lilian can be instanced. Spirits communicate without touching. The communion of the Orissers is beyond description and reason—it is a communion based on the instinct of an inner life, of like calling unto like. This idea of a communion transcending sense-communication was important to Myers. He knows well how to use the power of silence and stillness to evoke the ordered way of life of the Orissers—an attempt to relate the external scene to the inner life of the individual. Yet he realises that such tranquillity may lead to mere inertia—"this stillness brought melancholy to the heart." Eamor is the best that at the moment he can conceive of life as offering; but it provides only a temporary equilibrium fraught with certain dangers. Life there can too easily merge into indifference.

For it seemed that the sky and the earth and all hearts had lost their passion in that the world's energies lay buried for ever under sheer indifference.

Too great a development of the inner life can lead to stagnancy. And in Myers's constant evocation of scenes of tranquillity, the too frequent use of the pathetic fallacy, the inability to conceive any dynamic relationship between his characters and the ordinary everyday mundane things of life, a certain weakness is detectable. One feels, that is, that the scene too often is painted to fit the mood, rather than that the mood is evoked in relationship to the scene. The novel reveals a characteristic dichotomy of Myers's mind. The life of society with its permeating sexuality, its encouragement of the 'public' personality and its material self-glorification has to be rejected; humanistic at its best, it is still "miserably incomplete." There remain two alternatives: one is a scepticism, recognisably daemonic at bottom, based on the intellectual ego as the unescapable substrate, from which the only relief leads into stillness, void, disembodiment, through a conscious division of flesh and spirit; for the intellect destroys the life of colour and experience, as Nicholas's incapacity for relationship with Isobel goes to show.

The other solution emerges from 'a healthy turn of mind'—a realisation of the power of the material which avoids the superficial social self-glorification of the Maynes by recognising the deeper (almost cosmic) movements of organic life. The power of instinct belongs to this animal life of the race and with it the individual elements of the mind must be harmonised.

The danger is, as we have seen, that the relief of disembodiment will become merely stagnancy, 'a dreadful peace'; it is impossible to suppress the emotional life completely, as even Nicholas finds. On the other hand fellow-feeling, relationship with humanity, can so easily become merely humanistic—'love' dissociated from an enclosing faith; worse still, it partakes of that kind of idealised 'love' so acutely and persistently analysed by Lawrence, a sort of socialised benevolence hiding a bullying will, while a generalised feeling for humanity may make immediate personal relationships unnecessary—as Allen finds his relationship with Lilian ultimately inessential. Myers himself moved between 'rage and indifference,' as he states in a letter, between a feeling for life—the vague, cosmic life of the Great Mother, expressing a need for integration in the natural world—and a desire for 'escape' into a world of spirit. He was too conscious of the evil in it to be able to leave the world; such evil could not be ignored. But Nirvana was terribly tempting. This strongly negative aspect emerges in Myers's constant concern with stillness. Disillusionment wears a twin aspect. It was necessary, as a means of approach to Nirvana, to strip the veils of those illusions to which Bacon, in the epigraph to the novel, quoted above, refers; but once removed, there was revealed disillusionment in the other sense, that achieved by Nicholas, provoking a wearying irony towards existence.

The novel as a novel, as, that is to say, a work of art, is not successful; and it is now time to examine more closely the technique and method for they will reveal certain weaknesses in Myers's manner and outlook. His strength undoubtedly lay in the inner life; part of him, as Mr Walter Allen has said,[1] was 'intuitive' introvert and he found the true richness of life in an inner meaning. Though his grasp on externals became more sure as he grew older, his incapacity to convey 'felt life' in terms of concrete actualities always remains a weakness of his method and has militated against that recognition of his excellence which the sensitivity of his mind and vision merits. It is no accident that the foregoing analysis has been concerned chiefly with the mental processes, the 'thoughts', of the characters; it is these mental aspects of the different

[1] In an article in *Orion*.

persons of the drama that remain in the mind after the work has
been laid down. The great artist needs to have a keen eye for externals,
if only as symbolic representations of his inner feelings. Wordsworth,
with whom the early Myers had some affinity, in that both were interested ultimately only in the movements of their own minds, nevertheless managed to transmit his emotion and by doing so, to create an effect
of precision, by investing certain scenes, certain people, with a significance which helped to convey to us his attitude towards existence.
Admittedly we may not believe in the leech-gatherer quite as Wordsworth found him; but at least he serves as an adequate symbol which
embodies the emotion and makes it communicable. And we find that
all the finest writers have tended to follow Tchekov's advice about the
moonlight: "Cut out all those pages," he wrote to a friend who sought
advice, "about the moonlight, and give us instead what you feel about
it—the reflection of the moon in a piece of broken bottle."

Now Myers's sense of the outer world in this first novel is perfunctory,
and this fact is reflected in the style. His method is adequate for the
description of the purely intellectual movements of the mind. But
everything is stated, nothing is conveyed. Few of the incidents of the
novel have for the reader quite that validity with which Myers tries to
invest them. We find some difficulty in regarding the central situation
—the handing over of Eamor—as an adequate "objective correlative"
to the passions aroused, and many of the minor incidents fail almost
completely. For we feel that they have been manufactured to fit in with
the author's intellectual preconceptions, what he thinks the characters
'stand for'. It is this that explains the strange melodramatic atmosphere
that invests the whole work. Myers is incapable of conveying scenes
of passion, because he lacks the restraint that makes passion believable;
he forgets what Shakespeare in *King Lear* remembered—the 'buttons'
of life.[1] There is an attempt to infuse the central incident with a portentousness that it cannot maintain, to invest the struggle with a sense
of vast subterranean forces at work that would serve to make it convey
more than overtly it would seem to merit; and this fails. The emotionalism of the phrases which so constantly recur, "unearthly glitter,"
"dreadful laugh," etc., constitutes an effort to create a tension, to work
up a strength of feeling which nothing (as it is conveyed to us) in the
inner life of the characters goes to confirm. (The inner conflict of
Nicholas, for instance, except in his hatred of the Maynes, is on the
whole rationalistic.) What is genuine is the investigation into the world
of mind, the understanding of the subterfuges of personality, some of
the philosophical disquisition (the Jungian mysticism, however, wears a

---

[1] "Pray you, undo this button"—where the concrete effect gives actuality to the tre-
mendous scene of passion and torment at the end of the play.

pretty feeble look), and the capacity to correlate apparently disparate aspects of psychic being. Often the analyses—of Madeline, for instance—are magnificently penetrating. But there is also a certain failure in sympathy. The melodrama springs partly from an over-simplification of the problem—the characters are too extreme. Myers lacks that particular sort of ironic detachment possessed by such an author as, say, George Eliot, which enables the writer to see round a problem, to realise it in all its complexities and hence, while maintaining a sense of moral standards, to enter into a fuller sympathy—in itself part of what the writer has to offer in the direction of positive belief—with the situations of the characters. What feeling is present is crude and frequently worked up for the purpose. Even the quarrel between Madeline and Lilian, one of the best psychological incidents in the book, analytically, is marred in that the scene fails to make an emotional impact on the reader. One accepts it as a true analysis of the effect of one personality on another—but one's acceptance is almost completely intellectual. The situation is conveyed only in terms of the movements of Madeline's mind with, towards the climax, a rather obvious undercurrent of irony. The scene never crystallises into anything that would give it solidity; it finds nothing in the external world that would serve to anchor it and make it precise. Dostoievsky once said to a writer who had described the throwing of pennies to an organ man: "I want to hear that penny hopping and chinking." Nothing really hops and chinks in *The Orissers*.

It is interesting to compare Myers's method with that of Thomas Mann in *The Magic Mountain*. Both are writers of 'philosophical' novels and the outlook of both, with difference of stress, might be termed Liberal. Mann, however, reveals the philosophic import of his creation through a secure presentation of external symbols. What Hans Castrop (and the others) 'stand for' is conveyed not in explicit and conventional terms, by means of direct statement, or analysis, but by a translation into external facts and objects, of inner motivations and desires. Settembrini's constant appearance in his familiar check trousers and pilot coat is the concrete expression of the pedagogic repetitiveness of his humanist philosophy. Those tricks of manner and voice that Mann gives him seem to direct us towards certain abstract features of his philosophic output—in a word, he 'chinks'. *The Magic Mountain* itself, a symbol of the life of the middle-classes, may stand for a world of appearances, of deceptions to which the bourgeois mind is prone; but these 'appearances' take on a concrete expression in Mann's description of thermometers, weather, and meals (the last of which are described in a very detailed manner), and from these we judge the inner triviality. 'Eamor' as an expression of a certain way of life, at once refined and

weary, we have to accept in terms of statement; it has no independent
life of its own by which one might guess the significance it has for the
writer. The characters remain static—they possess no inner dynamism.
Myers's dislike of nineteenth-century rationalism is in itself a tribute,
perhaps, to the power that such a mode of apprehension had for him.
The whole presentation through argument, and the descriptions of the
processes of the characters' minds, with their logical deductions of
states of being from certain premises also tends to strengthen this unconscious tribute. He belongs to the Victorian tradition, not to that
newer mode of writing which works so largely through an intuitive
apprehension of Images, which convey without stating the 'notion' of
the writer. The intellectual discipline of his work is considerable, but it
emerges from the abstract analysis of the mind. In the case of George
Eliot, for instance, the analysis related itself to concrete happenings in
a manner which showed the workings of the mind in integral contact
with the stuff of everyday experience; her moralising emerges from
the 'action'. Her generalisations on childhood, in *The Mill on the Floss*,
grow out of a consideration of Maggie Tulliver's actual conduct—the
incidents are not constructed to fit in with a preconceived notion of
how children behave. This is not so with Myers. He, like Nicholas,
arrives at a realisation of the necessity of the spiritual life by processes
ultimately intellectual; and in the case of Nicholas, this understanding
does not emerge from a plenitude of concrete incidents leading to an
abstract understanding; the experience that lies behind such a mental
apprehension is perfunctory and ill-digested. It is worth noting that
Nicholas's idea of spirit is of a "conscious isolation" . . . "Spirits cannot unite." Therefore the life of the spirit really implies an intellectual
isolation that is respected by another: "Spirit communicates without
uniting." Again, Nicholas points out that intuition is a creation of the
intellect. Myers's sense of the power of feeling and emotion was based
on mind concepts of these things, and becomes talk about passion rather
than emotion conveyed.

One other point about *The Orissers* is worth noting; it is one which
involves an amplification and a refinement of what has already been
mentioned. Myers rarely wrote about places he had actually visited.
Only Eamor in this novel seems to bear a resemblance to any actual
environment he had encountered—the house, I am told, bears a certain
likeness to that of his father-in-law at Glen Eyrie in Colorado. Otherwise the location of the novel is quite imaginary. And just as the location is detached from actuality, so the characters themselves give a
curious effect of rootlessness. Although we are told that the Orissers
are an old family and that Eamor has been in their hands for many hun-
dreds of years, there is no sense, in Myers's handling of them, of any

continuity other than that involved in a perfunctory mention of, and a
certain emphasis, in describing the house and grounds, on, antiquity.
Despite their ancient lineage the Orissers are historically abstracted.
Eamor is described as a "backwater, a pool severed by drought from
the main stream." The Orissers come into no social contact with their
historical environment, in the way in which, for instance, Sebastian
does in Miss Sackville West's *The Edwardians*, which, though a less
important novel than *The Orissers*, does involve the predicament of the
hero in a historically defined context with its inevitable strains and
stresses as an essential element in the central conflict. Nor is there any
representative of an older generation—such as Mr Longden presents in
Henry James's *The Awkward Age* —to give point to the criticism of current manners and behaviour. The Orissers, in fact, are not only isolated
from business—the world of the Maynes—and, to a lesser degree, from
one another; they are also isolated from any continuity, any fineness
socially realised and still perceived from which their present state might
either draw sustenance or their inadequacies be more surely placed.
They exist within no world which, if only as an echo, can evoke a
social code or morality—which for a moralist is a serious situation.
For Myers seems too little aware of the egotism which exists at the
bottom of the Orissers' natures, which the incidents of the novel reveal,
and which a finer sensibility might possibly have allowed for more fully,
implicitly, if not explicitly. It is as if Myers, living a generation later than
Henry James (perhaps the last great novelist really in touch—to the
extent of consciousness—with a tradition) had failed to make contact
with any realised social fineness; he had apprehended only the brooding
disillusionments of those who, in a different context, might have provided more fully realised modes of good living integrated with the
life around them in terms of inherited ways and duties—touching
everyday 'vulgar' life at many points and refining its incidence. Their
isolation lacks even the moral strength and integration of Conrad's sea-
captains, who, within their world, are closely and inevitably bound up
with the moral success of a particular sort of social enterprise.

The difficulty of the Orissers, then, is that they are provided with
nothing external on which to exercise such moral integrity as they
possess; to enter the world of 'service' would have been to lay themselves open to the same corruptions to which the Maynes were liable—
it would merely provide a means of sustaining their own self-esteem
because of the power such a life would give them of meddling in the
affairs of others. But if the true life is *only* the one within—and it is a
dangerous conception for a novelist—such a life, as Myers presents it,
involves the negativism of isolation. At the end of the book Myers
evades the sentimentality which destroys *Howard's End* as a mature

presentation of a similar theme; he thus avoids the ambiguity inherent in the idea 'only connect'; but he has still only succeeded in presenting aspects of his problem. *The Orissers* is perhaps best regarded as a statement of themes. As Professor D. W. Harding pointed out in *Scrutiny* (June, 1937), Myers uses his more morally reputable characters as a means to raising genuine problems; they provide the media through which he explores the relationship between the individual consciousness and life in the larger sense. Eamor provides a temporary resting-place, a retreat that is at once an emancipation and a prison-house. The burden of self-consciousness must be accepted—Myers can conceive of no 'solution' in terms of more instinctive modes of life as can D. H. Lawrence. But on what terms is a civilised existence possible in a society as gross as that offered by the Standishes and the Maynes? The other novels are, in their various ways, nearly all related to his search for a solution; one feels that the solution mattered to him as a man, that it was intimately related to his own personal problem of aloneness, and that his suicide is a comment on the vision of perfect personal relationships which characterises his last work.

CHAPTER II

"THE 'CLIO'"

PURELY from a technical point of view, Myers's next novel, *The 'Clio'*, which first appeared in 1925, is a distinct improvement. It lacks the depth of *The Orissers*, but it also escapes the portentousness of the earlier work. The obtrusive melodramatic atmosphere, which tended to mar the previous novel, has been replaced by a much lighter touch. *The 'Clio'* was written during the most worldly period of Myers's life, partly in response to the challenge of writers like Aldous Huxley, to prove that he too was capable of the sophisticated trifle. At the same time, there is still an awareness, discernible more in occasional hints than in sustained investigation, of possible depths. But Myers has managed to distance, to stand aloof from, the whole series of events and to strike some sort of a balance between the inner and outer being of the characters. External factors begin to play a more important part; the more varied physical features of the setting provide by their independent existence a method, alternative to the prolonged psychological disquisition of *The Orissers*, of revealing the inner lives of the characters. *The 'Clio'* is in many ways the least significant of Myers's works. But it is perhaps a necessary prelude to the writing of a great novel.

There is a considerable change in the style. Standing detached from and in tone superior to, all his characters, Myers is able to give more play to observation. And though he is still not really capable of conveying a scene of passion—the parting of Harry and his mother is a scene that fails to come off—the relative superficiality of the story and of the relations between the characters gives more legitimate opportunity for stage management. There is constant variety in the flitting from one character to another; this provides an exercise in technique that is to stand him in good stead when he comes to *The Root and the Flower* with its constant succession of interwoven events, and the difficulties of manipulating the multifarious dignitaries of empire. In *The 'Clio'*, no character dominates the scene, no central conflict invites a prolonged study of reactions. Yet there is progression of a more varied sort than there was in *The Orissers*. Certain experiences are undergone, and as a result of these experiences, a change comes over the protagonists. And there is a theme—or perhaps a number of closely related themes—which suggests a more serious underlying intention than a superficial reading would suggest. If the standards of the Orissers are in abeyance, they are not totally forgotten: the two works are demonstrably by the same hand. And if the handling of certain foibles is more tolerant, the pervasive irony nevertheless is the sign of an awareness of other possibilities of existence, tacitly excluded but never forgotten. Underlying the world of appearances, of those self-conscious elegances with which the greater part of the book is concerned, are to be found sincerer emotions or more profound realities of action. And the bringing together of the sophisticated and the primitive, of the civilised and the primeval, reveals the possibilities of a deep sincerity.

For the theme of the novel is still that of appearance and reality, as, of course, was that of *The Orissers*. A device at least as old as the *Tempest* —perhaps as remote as *The Odyssey*—is used. There is a voyage, and the 'sea-change' that some of the characters undergo reveals the deeper possibilities of character under the sophisticated veneer. No great depths are exposed; but certain at least of the characters abandon the elaborate play-acting, the conscious performance of a frivolous ritual which mark their mode of existence at the beginning. A yachting party of wealthy people is travelling up the Amazon. In the effort to avoid some floating mines which a revolution in the neighbouring state has caused to be cast into the river's waters, the yacht is driven into the bank. Grounded there for some time, the characters, under the strain of their position react in various ways to the external situation (which comprises both the civil war and the particular opportunities afforded by the stretch of jungle they have been cast upon) and to each other. One dies; two join the revolution; new relationships are formed under the impulse towards self-knowledge that the situation evokes.

The social milieu is, then, again that of the rich—as with all Myers's work. The 'Clio' is "probably the most expensive steam-yacht in the world"; she is well-groomed, freshly painted, and arrogant. No plan marks her voyage—she is the subject of caprice. Here are collected in an atmosphere consciously artificial the elegant denizens of a sophisticated civilisation going through the self-conscious but still socially articulated motions of living. These are the Maynes, without their grossness, preserving a certain standard. The sense that dominates is a tactile one. It is the feel of places that Myers is beginning to depict; the oppressive clamminess of a steam-heated jungle and the luxuriance of tropical vegetation are adequately evoked.

On the ship are Lady Oswestry and her two sons, Harry, Lord Oswestry, and Hugo. There is Sir James, her friend, the man she would marry. There are the young women, Angela, Mary, and Olga, engrossed either in their affairs or in the adornment of their bodies. If Stella Barlow adds a more serious tone, it is more than counterbalanced by the triviality of Francis Tilling. And there are the officers in charge of the boat, the doctor, and the crew. It is indeed the description of the

crew that first crystallises our sense of the author's detachment. Odd
remarks such as

They made the silent, coolly-tinted cabin seem like an aquarium tank, in
which mistress and maid were a silver and a dark-hued fish,

and the description of the smell at the lunch table, "the smell of the fine
flower of civilisation," had already warned us of a certain undercurrent
of criticism implicit in the observation. The description of the sailors
defines this:

Looking down on the concertina player and his fellows . . . one could not
help but liken them to prize pigs in a sty. And the comparison was all to their
advantage, for they looked happier and more intelligent than pigs. They were
fat, it is true, but not unhealthy. If they ate well it was because they were able to
digest well. What class is better able to assimilate nourishing food than sailors?
Sea air stimulates metabolism, the appetite responds, the vigorous liver co-
operates, the healthy mind reflects the vacancy of the circumambient horizon;
there is everything to promote and nothing to impede the enormous digestive
capacities which the sea develops in her children. All mammals that take to a
sea life acquire girth and placidity; witness the whale, the sea-elephant, and the
dugong or sea-cow. As for the *Clio's* crew—well! look at those buttocks! look
at that forearm and especially at the back of that neck! Mark closely that neck!
The necks of able-bodied seamen on expensive yachts well repay a careful study.
Measure the breadth and compare it first with the breadth of the back of the
head and, secondly with the breadth of the forehead. Prod it next with your
finger and note the peculiar resiliency. Observe the deep rich colour, examine
the grain of the skin. Necks such as this tell their simple story with conciseness
and eloquence.
On this portion of the deck and within these lumps of brick-red flesh amazing
feats of digestion and assimilation were being accomplished. These worthy
fellows, lying about like seals on a floe, looked inactive, but in truth they were
not. And if one of them belched occasionally, it was done out of pure sociability.

One is struck by the greater wealth of observation, the keener eye for
externals manifested, for example, in the remark about buttocks and
the necks. There is nothing like this in *The Orissers*. If the style is still
consciously literary, it has gained in flexibility. And the description of
the outward scene is used deliberately as a means of directing the
reader's attention to the significance of the whole of which the sailors
form part. The conscious irony explicitly comments on the type of life
that engenders such a scene; the comradely belch reverberates in the
more elegant luncheon room above the deck—it is the proletarian
counterpart, as it were, of the delicate aroma wafted by the punkah.
The servants—stewards, ladies' maids—revelling in obscenity and vulgarity when on their own, suggest a further commentary on the
ordered standards of their masters and mistresses. The yachting party,

if less physically gross, is nevertheless, by implication and explicit comment, subjected to a similar ironic scrutiny.

And yet the irony is not unkind. These people, it seems to suggest, may be futile and superficial, their existence may be concerned with trivialities, and their world bounded by face creams and bath salts, their relationships strained by the underground effluences of sex-consciousness and its accompanying self-awareness and consequent subtle rivalries. Nevertheless, as a social group they are aware of "certain standards to keep up"; and like the doctor, Myers may be said to be not "at all sure that civilisation (in the ordinary and slightly gross sense of the word) wasn't the best thing in the world." At least his attitude, if detached, is not wholly unsympathetic. These people stand for something. They share with the Orissers, if nothing else, at least one kind of awareness.

Nevertheless at the first it is their triviality that is emphasised. Their position is one of conscious isolation. "The sea offers a glorious relief from responsibility"—and the relaxation is partly Myers's as well as that of his characters. Their isolation is from past and future—but, and here lies the significance, the present may, because of the receptivity engendered, bring forth anything. If the Amazon they are approaching performs no other function it may force an attention on the vacancy of their minds. They are all, in their various ways, consciously concerned with superficialities, with play-acting. To Lady Oswestry, "too intelligent a woman to cultivate philosophic pretensions" (is that ironic? —one is not quite certain; this is perhaps Myers on the rebound) the most important thing in life is her face cream, which "an idiotic little revolution" may prevent her from getting at Para, and without which her chances of marrying Sir James in order to aid her son, Hugo's, career, would become more remote. For externals have their importance and she does not make the "mistake of imagining that Sir James prized beauty less for having reached the age to know that it was skin deep." Mary is undergoing the pangs of a love affair which seems to have no assured basis in community of feeling, but which is tormenting her nevertheless. Hugo, whose career is being arranged, and Stella, biographer of Lenin and "sentimental revolutionary," are emerging from an unsatisfactory love affair, Hugo tormented by his moral sense and Stella by memories of her husband. Angela, secure in the possession of the most amusing lingerie on board, "frivolously feminine," has plenty of scope for exercising her dominating interest in life, "her regard for appearances." Knowing well the necessity of displaying the right tastes as well as the right clothes, she furnishes her mind with titbits of cultural and literary knowledge gleaned from the pages of a fortnightly fashion magazine. Olga, more self-critical, has nevertheless a certain brazenness and is at the moment pretending a passion for Harry. Sir James, one of the more mature figures, has achieved a certain inner stability, though at a cost. By a conscious policy of disregarding his own finer feelings and by investing the frivolous and the trivial with a spurious significance, he is, in the end, enabled to achieve the desired poise—based on a lack of inner conflict. Only Harry, conscious buffoon actuated by an intense vanity, a "born comedian, a man who could do anything for the sake of effect," yet rejects the standards of this civilisation and, having refused to settle down to a serious career in England, is half comically, half seriously, directing a revolution in Amazonia. The picture of Harry, incidentally, is a particularly good one—the realisation of the essential element of irresponsibility and buffoonery needed in the modern dictator, of the underlying element of savage comedy which has revealed itself in the events of the last thirty years, was a considerable stroke of prescience. For Harry represents the elements of conscious fraud, the rejection of civilised standards such as they are and above all the contempt for his dupes—the pantomime element, in a word, of the modern European Great Man. Stella and Mr Wilkinson, who joins the ship later, are, for all their concern for social conditions, sentimentalists. Hugo is too doctrinaire, too concerned with first principles. Harry, as Sir James opines, is "your true politician and leader of men."

It is when they are brought into contact with other possible ways of life that the better side of these somewhat vapid creatures is displayed. While anchored off Para, they are joined by two others, Professor Brown and Mr Wilkinson (the commonplace nature of the names is significant). Mr Wilkinson, suffering from dysentery, has, while rowing out to the ship, received a call that no man disobeys. He has therefore sought refuge on board the 'Clio', where he is later followed by his puzzled friend, the Professor. The finding of Mr Wilkinson in the lavatory is another of those grosser physical details that comments upon the constipated life of the others; for they, like the heroines of Driffield in Mr Somerset Maugham's *Cakes and Ale*, are totally devoid of back passages. But it also introduces Mr Wilkinson in an absurd light—and this he never loses. The Professor is admitted to be a "darling old duck"; he is purely the conventional professor of fiction who boils the watch and holds the egg in his hand. His interest is in *lepidoptera* and not in human beings. But Mr Wilkinson is a figure who merits more attention; he is a preliminary sketch for Smith, the humanist of *The Root and the Flower*, a type that Myers particularly disliked. With him love is a principle and not an instinct, and his liking is proportionate to the distance between himself and the subject. For he exhibits all the self-consciousness of the class-conscious 'progressive' University type. "All ease of manner affects him as showiness," Sir James diagnoses; and Wilkinson combines a distaste for wealth as such with an intellectual snobbery of a peculiarly restricted kind—that nourished by a University community with its standards which spring from an awareness of self and its private jokes. It is in contrast to Mr Wilkinson, altruistic but dry, learned but even when compared to an ordinary sailor not really intelligent, that Sir James shows his finer standards. Mr Wilkinson's social sympathy is based only on an inverted snobbery, whereas Sir James's feelings spring from a genuine regard for his equals. For as Hugo considers:

> The honour of the human race was safer in that man's hands, his selfishness, hardness, and cynicism notwithstanding. He [Hugo] had an intuition that Sir James's materialism was impregnated with idealism, while the concealed foundation of Mr Wilkinson's idealism was, he judged, materialistic.

The Amazonians, the only other people who appear in the novel, again present no alternative standard to that of the yachting party. Unlike Mr E. M. Forster, whose Italians and Indians, for instance, though far from perfect, do offer a serious criticism of the falsity and hypocrisy of English middle-class life, in terms of gaiety, spontaneity, and community of feeling, or D. H. Lawrence, who found in more primitive races a genuineness of emotional response, an inner vitality which compared favourably with the deadness of 'civilised' existence, Myers offers no such alternative. The Amazonians are typified by the little man who is worrying whether a pink form ought not to be used instead of a yellow one; the comment, with which one feels Myers agrees, is Sir James's:

> The things we get excited about are, I think, more important things; although of course we couldn't very well explain why we get excited about them, or even *why* they are important. But we can point to European civilisation and say to that man: "People like you couldn't have built it up, and couldn't even keep it going although we have shown you the way."

However inadequate the Oswestrys and their company may be, the Amazonians are even more useless; they are absurd, and their revolution takes on, as Harry says, a musical comedy aspect. When they are not comic they are either incompetent or disgusting. Joachim, the Paranese pilot, guiding the boat more by good luck than good management, or announcing the blowing up of the 'Tigre'—"People all in little bits. All bloody and 'orrible. You not like to come and see?"—represents them adequately.

This unwillingness to consider in the more primitive race an alternative standard is interesting when one compares Myers with his contemporaries, for it demonstrates how rational his approach was. It shows, too, how much elegance, order, and some of the more sophisti-cated social graces appealed to him at this time. It also provides a fur-ther indication of his distaste for emotional exuberance. There is no realisation of good fellowship in any gross sense—except occasionally for ironic purposes—where Myers is concerned. He was, to use a key word of his, too 'fastidious'. It was at the time he wrote The 'Clio' that his acceptance by the artistic and social circles of London induced those feelings of superiority and snobbishness to which reference is made in the biographical chapter.

Nevertheless the primitive does play a part in his thought as it does in this novel. But it is typically the primitive of "silence and slow time." The "dreadful peace of Eamor" is here replaced by the jungle and swamps of Amazonia, an external setting which provides more than a mere background. For that relationship between internal and external that Myers was seeking and failed to find in The Orissers is here more subtly conveyed. The sunset that affects Sir James so powerfully with apprehensions of death is an indication of a better integration; and the effect of the jungle is pervasive. The arrogance of the ship is nullified. What was in the Atlantic so free and self-confident becomes "a little white tub, the tops of her funnels being on a level with what looked like low bushes on the bank." Life assumes a different proportion and death comes to take on a different aspect. There is a sense of sinister concentration of forces, of an alien subjection. For Hugo "human be-ings and forests and sunsets were all part of a sad and insoluble mystery." Nevertheless it is obvious that Myers is still seeking to convey an emotional intensity which is beyond his powers. For he only succeeds in describing the forest to us—he never conveys it as, for instance, Conrad would have done. There is no real distinguishing quality of style, no slight distortion of effect such as Thomas Mann uses to convey the sense of a rise in temperature involved in an ascent to The Magic Moun-tain. There is a failure in emotional concentration. Nevertheless the effect of the jungle is given in incident and straightforward descrip-tion; it provides the testing-time for the characters. If there is no trans-mutation into something "rich and strange," certain potentialities are revealed and certain more satisfactory modes of existence explored.

The immediate causes of the trouble are a couple of mines. The revolutionaries, fearing the approach of a hostile gun-boat, the 'Tigre', have mined the river, with half a dozen mines stolen off a warship from last year's Guy Fawkes' day. Harry, noticing the mines just in time, pulls the boat into the side of the river, where she sticks in the mud. Despite all efforts, the incompetence of the natives and the appearance of the 'Tigre' prevent the necessary relaunching, and the 'Clio' is held up for several weeks. And so the ship "had been taken as an unwilling neophyte into the penetration of the God of Amazonia." The physical subjection of the vessel to its surroundings is emphasised. The tempo of the Jungle imposes itself upon the tempo of civilised social life. The attempt to keep up appearances becomes unmistakably an effort; the logic of the jungle asserts itself. Some it affects no more than with a faint uneasiness, a greater consciousness of boredom. Francis, for instance, is quite untouched—even his chattering continues: his triviality is on such a magnificent scale that it almost merits respect. He returns to life unchanged and we may abandon him to his cheerful fatuity and his shrinking bank balance.

But on most of the others a new sense of reality asserts itself, a shift in relationships takes place, superficialities are exposed, deeper issues faced. Life when brought up against the alien standard of the jungle, with its massive unconcern for human self-consciousness, takes on a sterner aspect and demands the assertion of those standards of behaviour implicit but undeveloped, in the finer consciousness of the members of the party. Particularly is this so in the case of Sir James and of Hugo and Mary.

To Sir James the jungle brings death. It is in the face of death that Sir James acts up to those standards which have been inherent in his worldliness. Although he has been unable to summon up any vague humanitarian sympathy for those with whom he is not brought into contact, but has believed in the rule of the rich for the rich, he has always manifested a certain genuineness in personal relationships. It is a genuineness based on an appreciation of his own superficiality—for Sir James has followed the Greek injunction 'Know thyself'. Self-knowledge has led him to avoid close contacts and produced a certain light-heartedness in his estimation of others. Always in search of the frivolous, as he has grown older, he has not allowed anyone to make an insistent demand on him; as a young man he always desired to keep his amours light and superficial. His self-awareness and increased self-control have led him to avoid too close an entanglement with Lady Oswestry and to embark on a mildly lecherous affair with Angela. To this conscious policy of avoiding emotional entanglement he now adheres even at the hour of his death. For he remains true to his own superficiality which now manifests itself not only in a willingness to avoid such entanglements but in a desire to save others from emotional disturbance. If his attitude previously has led to a certain loneliness in life, he accepts that aloneness as a condition of dying. He avoids, in fact, the worst feature of all invalids, self-pity, "renouncing even the relief of an occasional groan," and paradoxically attains, as a result of those very qualities which by more rigorous standards would be marks of his unfitness to live, a certain dignity and approved worth in dying. If he has lived a life of externals, it is in externals that this limited consideration for others manifests itself; he will not permit an expression of suffering even to be seen on his face. And in terms of his own superficial philosophy he attains a certain inner peace and dignity at the end.

On Hugo the impact of the jungle is different. Dissatisfied with the progress of his affair with Stella, and afflicted by moral scruples about breaking it off, he seeks the peace and quiet of the surrounding forest. He is bitten by a snake, however, and his resulting terror drives away his previous *weltschmerz*, induced by the feeling of contrast between the transitory nature of man's existence and the permanence of the forest. Now, to live becomes his dearest wish. Thinking himself lost, he is at last forced to sit, exhausted, on the ground, where he prepares himself for death. There he is found by Mary and in the resulting scene, both his previous depression and his terror seem illusory. For both he and Mary achieve an access of strength through love, and Hugo comes to understand "that what really mattered was the emotional reality at which one lived." Their feeling for each other, their certainty as to reciprocity of affection, lifts their lives on to another plane. Both discover the falsity of their previous loves, both lose (though the words are applied to Hugo only) "the good thick skin, the work-a-day sanity, the robust independence of those who do not love." The sense of the sanctity of human relationship based on the deepest feelings, not yet however invested with any transcendental value, nevertheless foreshadows the understanding between Mohan and Damayanti in *The Pool of Vishnu*. Here at least, in a world of semi-illusions, is something genuine, some touchstone of experience by which the work-a-day world can be judged and found—characteristically in this work of equivocation—both despicable and enviable.

The others suffer similar readjustments. Stella and Harry accept the challenge to the sentimentalities of their revolutionary ardours. They leave the 'Clio' for Para to the sound of firing from the town. For Lady Oswestry, the time of renunciation has come; with the loss of Sir James, she enters on the last stage of a woman's existence, "unsupported by the expectation of a love affair," a comment which very clearly exposes the superficiality of her existence. And she loses her son, Harry. But it is a renunciation that achieves a certain dignity; true to her own nature, she makes no appeal based on self-pity; in both her case and that of Sir James it is a renunciation that is accepted despite the bitterness engendered. Olga has to take the consequences—or what she imagines are the consequences—of her own prudery. Hugo, she thinks, has preferred Stella, in the past, because Stella has the secret of coming to grips with life. She does not realise that her failure is a mark of her own greater power of self-criticism, and that her pluck, as Myers comments, is no less than Stella's. Only Angela (and Francis) are quite untouched; and in that they also remain true to their inner selves; for, as Harry comments, "it is not a sin but triviality that hideth us from God"; and their inability to achieve happiness or suffering is a reassertion of their vapidity, the final irony of their worthlessness.

The novel, then, is not lacking in awareness; yet, as has been said, it is the least significant of Myers's works. For the book is based subconsciously on an ambivalence of which the pervasive irony is the outward manifestation. Its main characteristics are a greater light-heartedness, a more conscious detachment and superficiality, which result in an appearance of tolerance. If, it seems to question, these people are not wholly satisfactory, where can be found a substitute? And when they are subjected to a test they do in the main respond in a manner which at least is a tribute to breeding (Myers does not employ the word, but it sums up his attitude); they are capable of some feeling, if it is only a socialised concern for appearances. The irony becomes less marked as the book proceeds; the occupants of the scratched and damaged 'Clio', which seeks once more the waters of the Atlantic, have achieved a response to circumstances that demands at least a tribute to conscious effort. There is none of the self-conscious flippancy of, say, *Crome Yellow*. Myers has made the best of his world. Indeed, one knows that at times he enjoyed it. The desire to understand has been replaced by the desire to accept; and yet, inherent in the acceptance, as a tribute to intelligence, there is a critical appreciation of insufficiency which has led the author to dominate his material, consciously to 'place' and manipulate his effect. Technically, at least, the book marks an advance —that, it is to be hoped, has been made clear. What is wanted now is a novel which will embody the new resources of the novelist in a theme which allows the same depth of penetration as was to be found in *The Orissers*.

CHAPTER III

"THE ROOT AND THE FLOWER"

A. "THE NEAR AND THE FAR"

The Root and the Flower[1] is undoubtedly Myers's masterpiece. Published as a whole in 1935 it comprises three shorter works, *The Near and the Far* (1929), *Prince Jali* (1931), and *Rajah Amar*. It may lack the flexibility of tone and artistry of Forster's work, and the capacity to catch the evanescence of the perceptions in which lay much of the strength of Virginia Woolf; but it may well be judged superior to the works of both in seriousness of moral intent and depth of spiritual insight. Seriousness of purpose does not, of course, always result in significance of result; but in *The Root and the Flower* there is a moral solidity, a comprehensive effort after integrity, and a rejection of sham and illusion—in a word, a sustained search for truth which is translated into an assured artistic creation.

The setting is historical; the action takes place in the time of Akbar, the Great Mogul, who reigned from 1556 to 1605. Nevertheless, as Myers explains in his Preface, it is not to be regarded as an historical novel. Only four of the characters bear the names of actual historical characters—Akbar himself, Salim and Daniyal (the Emperor's two sons), and Shaik Mobarek. For the rest, fact has been distorted or ignored as the author's purposes required. To a critic friend he writes: "I don't think I can obviate the anachronistic modernity of certain conversation. I am afraid that blemish must remain." (Letter to Mr L. P. Hartley, 7 July 1929.) A scene remote from the world of to-day and from those political catch-words and shibboleths which might well arouse local passion and distract the reader from truths deeper than those associated with the purely temporary exigencies of policy was what Myers required; and sixteenth-century India provided him with this. The problems of Empire, the sense of great issues (great, that is to say, in the worldly sense), the colour and glitter, the pomp and circumstance of worldliness afforded him a setting adequately comprehensive to give significance to the spiritual and moral problems which his characters had to face. In *The Orissers*, with which *The Root and the Flower* most nearly invites comparison, one of the faults lay in the fact

---

[1] This account of the book is based on the final version. Myers wrote the first two parts, *The Near and the Far* and *Prince Jali*, separately. When he printed them together with *Rajah Amar* as *The Root and the Flower* he made some slight alterations in the earlier versions.

that the central conflict was concerned with issues too local, not sufficiently extensive in their implications, to warrant quite the force of moral and spiritual energy engendered (though it may be urged that more was at issue than appeared in the surface agitation and that the conflict had a symbolical import which extended beyond the immediate outcome). In addition, the moral question involved tended to be over simplified (as it is conveyed through the conflicts of the characters). This is not so in *The Root and the Flower*. The political issues—the mutual relationships of Akbar and his two sons involve the fate of India—are of a kind at least to balance the more personal concerns of the individual characters. For the ethical problems of private existence take on a wider significance when seen in their effects on imperial policies and dynastic relationships. And though the emphasis is still on the individual situation, *The Root and the Flower* is also a political novel, and the tergiversations of political action, the influence of political power or of the exercise of political tact on personality, form one, if only one, of the major interests of the novel. Such aspects comprise Myers's later and more mature investigation into the worldliness of the Maynes; and the problems involved are essentially modern problems.

Again, the situations are seen in all the ramifications of their complexities. The relationship between public and private life, for instance, raises issues that cannot be and are not reduced to a formula. The contact between the 'sensitive' and the 'vulgar,' dismissed as an impossibility in *The Orissers*, is seen in the later novel to involve responsibilities that the 'sensitive' cannot merely ignore. Myers, of course, is primarily interested in the individual's predicament in this political and social world. He is not concerned with the effect of political action on the masses of the people but only with its repercussion on the individual mind. Thus his choice, as a setting, of sixteenth-century India, with its essentially aristocratic system, is justified. But it must not be thought that the individuals whom he examines are exclusively or even always primarily subject to political drives and urges. Their philosophical pretensions, their relations not only to their society but to the cosmos and to one another, form the subject of his investigations, as in *The Orissers*. And here, in view of the strictures passed on *The Orissers*, a word must be said about the novel as a form of expression.

Virginia Woolf, in her essay on George Meredith in *The Second Common Reader*, has commented:

When philosophy is not consumed in a novel, and when we can underline this phrase with a pencil and cut out that exhortation with a pair of scissors and paste the whole thing in a system, it is safe to say that there is something wrong with the philosophy or with the novel or with both.

It is obvious that Myers felt a possible objection to his work, a criticism that would be framed in some such terms as these:

The suspicion may come into the reader's mind, *he says in his* Preface, that what he has before him is a philosophical novel, one in which the characters are abstractions personified: And if that is the case, he will say, the book can hardly be worth reading either as a novel or as philosophy.

In answer to any such challenge he points out that philosophical speculation forms an essential part of human nature and that to ignore such questions as rise to the lips of every child is "to become satisfied with art that is petty, reasoning that is pedantic, and knowledge that is not bread but a stone." He reveals that his philosophical interests have an ethical foundation, and it is this which provides his defence for the introduction of so much philosophical speculation among his characters. Philosophy to Myers was not something divorced from living—a fact which explains much of his contempt for the academic philosopher. All men must at some time, however fleeting, ask themselves questions about the ultimate purposes of the universe; and though, like Pilate, most do not stay for an answer, the urge towards some sort of philosophical speculation, however rudimentary, is endemic in the human condition. If, as may be allowed, the novelist's concern is with 'life' to restrict him from demonstrating certain aspects of existence that are as 'natural' to some people as sexual relations appear to be (a theme of which the novelists are not noticeably shy) is to limit arbitrarily, and with no good reason, the scope of the novel. No one can deny that a novelist is concerned with human conduct; and whereas conduct implies action, no one has denied the novelist the right to examine the psychological motives for action. That a man should act—that all men do in fact act—in accordance with certain views of existence and of their place in the scheme of things, whether openly expressed or covertly implied, is undeniable. And what Myers does is only an extension of what every novelist does; he explains the conduct of his characters in terms more of conscious philosophical preconceptions than of subconscious psychological urges; a man may just as well commit a murder in accordance with a certain intellectual moral code—Raskolnikov does—as for money, though perhaps such philosophical killing is less common.

Myers is, as we have seen, much concerned with problems of conduct, and the basis from which conduct springs. Moral rather than aesthetic sensibility is what he cares about. The moral basis of his dislike of certain petty forms of aestheticism is revealed, for instance, in his analysis of the unpleasant crew who surround Daniyal in this novel; what he particularly dislikes is that form of aestheticism which serves its devotees as an excuse for disregarding, taking up an attitude of superiority towards, any form of moral compulsion. "Emancipation" has produced a moral void, in an age noteworthy for its "spiritual vulgarity," its failure in moral sensibility. There has been too extreme a reaction against a period when 'conduct' admittedly attracted too much attention and perhaps stifled other potentialities of existence. Connoisseurs of 'character' are rare, almost non-existent; and character, to Myers, means moral integrity, a living based on the deepest spiritual and philosophical insight of which men are capable. Myers himself is such a connoisseur. He appreciates the need of restrictions on 'experience' in much the same way as Henry James does in *Roderick Hudson*. That novel, too, is concerned with the relation between the aesthetic sensibility demanding complete freedom of 'experience' and the claims of the moral sensibility, and Rowland's query as to whether men of Roderick Hudson's "large easy power" deserve an "ampler moral law than . . . narrow mediocrities like himself" receives a decided negative in the issue of the novel.

At the end of Myers's quest exists the idea that truth is and can be found. At the same time, he seems to have approved, for a time, the idea that philosophy is partly a question of temperament. But such an idea does not produce the moral chaos it might well have done, even though there is admittedly a slight confusion of thought. If it allows him to approve of certain characters who hold somewhat differing outlooks, and keep the balance fairly evenly between them, such approval is based on the depth of spiritual insight, the true knowledge of the workings of his own character to which each individual has attained, and the relationship of that character to the external world. The novel, that is to say, attains a uniformity of moral grasp that aids its coherence as a work of art. There may be more than one road to Nirvana, but that does not mean to say that any road will reach there or that a moral democracy is possible. If temperament leads the pilgrim along one road rather than another, that temperament has to be guided by a fastidious moral integrity which springs from the being's deepest sanction and corresponds to the profoundest spiritual resources of the universe. In any case, Myers as a novelist does not seek a philosophical *system*; he explores through his various characters the qualities of human conduct, in a manner proper to a novel.

Again, and this is the important point when considering possible criticisms of *The Root and the Flower* as a novel, these philosophical speculations of Myers's characters are in no way divorced from their conduct in the world of men—they act in accordance with their ethical preconceptions; and new potentialities of being are revealed to them in their contacts with others and in the behaviour invited or forced upon them by events. One of the criticisms urged above against *The Orissers* has been that the events had sometimes a factitious character—they appeared to have been manufactured to illustrate the required theme. No such criticism can, by and large, be made against the later novel. The manipulation of events is done with considerable skill; the situations which arise reveal, as in life itself, flaws in outlook or opportunities for an exercise of personal integrity. Some new aspect of character is exposed or some former intuition confirmed. Even so slight an incident as that provoked by the negligence of Daniyal in visiting Amar's father, the aged Rajah Bihar, is sufficient to bring out essential differences in the attitudes of Hari and Amar and, more important, reveals certain flaws in Amar's self-sufficiency. Sometimes, too, an incident will serve to focus, by its suddenness and violence, the response which a particular character has evoked. When Daniyal steps on the cat's head, he not only provides, from a technical point of view, an excellent and dramatic climax to the novel; he also crystallises in a single incident all one's feelings of revulsion, all one's apprehensions of the evil inherent in his nature. The petty yet revolting cruelty of the act is the open expression of an inner corruption of spirit.

There is an incident at the beginning of the book which, microcosmically, seems to bring into significant relationship the opposed worlds of 'being' and 'becoming' with which the book deals. Little Prince Jali, son of Rajah Amar and Sita, Amar's Christian wife, is leaning over the balcony of the great palace at Agra and is reminded of the scene from his father's palace at home. How exquisite had seemed the desert as one gazed at it from a distance; how tedious had a journey across its sandy wastes been in actual fact. Yet

He clung to the truth of appearances as something equal to the truth of what underlay them. There were two deserts: one that was a glory for the eye, another that it was a weariness to trudge. Deep in his heart he cherished the belief that some day the near and the far would meet.

So he looks forward to the occasion when he will be old enough to grasp "the magic of things seen afar," to realise the visionary scene before it can transform itself.

The idea of the 'near' and the 'far' is one that obviously was important to Myers. It is the title he gives to the first part of *The Root and the Flower*, and when *The Root and the Flower* and its sequel, *The Pool of Vishnu*, are published together, it is the title he gives to the whole work. Jali's consideration expresses in miniature the theme of the book. Mankind reaches out to a state of visionary blessedness that all too frequently is obliterated by the irritations and checks of daily life as we pass through the desert of existence. How often, like the snake which Jali sees strike at the insubstantial twigs and over-balance, are we deceived by some irrelevant consideration which exposes the weaknesses of our situation and involves us in hurt. The 'near' is ever present with its frequent irrelevances, in whose coils we are caught; the 'far' seems to recede as we seek it. Yet the far exists—there *is* a state which can be attained and in which appearance and reality can coalesce in true human actuality; though all too frequently the ultimate appearance—reality is as remote and as hard of access as Jali is to find it in his life's pilgrimage. Before he reaches it in front of the Pool of Vishnu, he has to shed many of the false appearances and illusions which strew his way through life.

Thus Myers, through incident and symbol, 'consumes' the philosophy he has to offer and submits his speculations to the demands of the novel. Direct exposition of philosophic position exists, but only in the way in which other writers would employ less intellectual indications of the motivations of their characters; the characters in Myers's book are what they are and act in the way they do because they are actuated by certain philosophic considerations. Those considerations can even be shown to be insufficient to guide conduct—as in the case of Gokal, who throws over his views in what he considers to be their inadequacy, so as to indulge himself in his relationship with Gunevati; such a departure from self-consciousness is not, however, shown to be successful.

When the story opens—the account that follows is based partly on Myers's own summary that he gave in his introduction to *The Pool of Vishnu*—the Emperor Akbar is not an old man, but his health is deteriorating and his two sons, Salim and Daniyal, are already intriguing to secure the succession. To stand aloof from this contest becomes increasingly difficult; and Amar, Rajah of Vidyapur, is confronted with the problem of which side to support. A Buddhist, he has for some years wished to retire to a monastery; he is only held back by concern for his wife, Sita, a Christian, for whom he still has a strong affection, though differences of outlook have tended to separate them, and for his young son, Jali, whose 'education', in the sense Henry Adams gives to the word, forms one of the focal points of the book. These three, together with the Brahmin Gokal, and to a limited extent, Hari Khan, chieftain of a small state, form the Orisser group in the book—those who, in their different ways, are self-consciously aware of perfection.

Sita has taken Hari Khan as a lover. Hari is married to Ambissa, a sister of Amar and a partisan of Prince Daniyal, who is trying to persuade Amar to join the prince's side. Ambissa hates her husband, though this fact does not affect the friendship of Hari and Amar. Before falling in love with Sita, Hari has had a clandestine affair with the daughter of an important chieftain, Makh Khan. This girl, Princess Lalita, is betrothed to Prince Daniyal, whom she hates. Prince Daniyal spends most of his time at the Pleasance of the Arts, a mountain retreat where he and his sophisticated friends have collected a crew of bogus actors and artists. The meretricious nature of this camp is seen as it reveals itself through the eyes of the young Jali, part of whose advance in knowledge of the world it forms. Among the players is Gunevati, a low-caste girl, at one time beloved of Gokal, who makes her escape to the Pleasance after an attempt to poison the Brahmin. Gunevati is in possession of secrets important to Mabun Das, Chief of Akbar's secret police, who, while loyal to the Emperor, is secretly antagonistic to Daniyal, for he favours Salim. Daniyal discovers these facts, lures Mabun Das to the Pleasance and there throws him into prison. Gunevati has her tongue cut out to prevent her speaking.

Chance brings Amar and Daniyal into contact; hatred of the Prince is one of the emotions that Amar nourishes but refuses to recognise in himself, so that politically he still tends to favour Daniyal on the grounds of expediency. Amar's decision to retire thus contains a flaw, for subconsciously at least he has not succeeded in freeing himself from the passions of the world. While Gokal is explaining the unsatisfactory nature of this decision to retire to Amar, a summons from Daniyal arrives. Daniyal, while simulating friendliness, taunts Amar with his wife's unfaithfulness, and Amar lays his hand upon his sword. An attendant strikes the Rajah down, and Gokal is forced to take him in an unconscious condition to a house where Sita, Hari, and Jali are awaiting his return. It is at this crucial moment, when Amar by his instinctive action has reasserted the claims of moral action in society, that the novel ends.

The first section of the trilogy is largely taken up with introducing the reader to the political situation, as one aspect of the phenomenal world. The love affairs of Hari and that of Gokal and Gunevati provide opportunities for comment on the theme of right relationships between individuals, a theme which comes to exercise Myers increasingly. This book, therefore, is mostly concerned with immediacy of experience, whether political or amorous, and the attempts of the main characters to achieve an ordered mode of life which will offer adequate concessions at once to the world around them and to their own personal integrities. Only Amar stands aside; and even he is politically involved.

The opposition between the phenomenal world of the immediate present in all its potential beauty and yet its transience, its corruption, and frequent underlying evil, and the more remote and detached states of mind to attain which involves discipline and sacrifice, a freedom from Maya, is then one of the themes of the book; the 'appearances' of the world are shown to contain many inadequacies when brought into contact with deeper spiritual 'realities'. Nevertheless, the implied opposition is one which perhaps introduces too fundamental a cleavage between the 'world' and the 'spirit', where the more spiritually aware characters are concerned, to do justice to the complexity of the treatment. For those who are aware of this opposition in effect offer, or come to offer, their concessions to both; they are those who recognise imperfection and aim at perfection; they are the spiritually awake, in fact, whose apprehension of certain values in the universe is a sufficient mark of difference from—of superiority to—the trivial and complacent. But they do not necessarily turn their backs on the world; and the one who does, Amar, wakes up later to inadequacy. The 'moral' we arrive at is that 'ordinary' worldly existence must be spiritualised, accepted on the level of 'reality' not on that of 'appearance'. The actions of everyday life need to be seen in relationship to extra-human standards and pervaded by their spirit; for those who seek such standards, in whatever differing ways, form a coherent group in aspiration. Much of this, however, belongs to the later volumes; the first is much taken up with the cult of appearances, with the great world.

Gokal exposes an essential 'division'—an expression in terms which are reminiscent of, but profounder than, the cleavage of the Orissers and the Maynes—when he points out to Sita that, despite differences of temperament and outlook, she and Amar are fundamentally of the same type; and they are so because they are bound together by a search for spiritual values; in their seeking, they stand over against the 'trivial', worldly characters:

"I, for my part, shall always affirm what Amar denies. Between us there is a gulf."

Gokal leaned forward earnestly. "The gulf lies not between those who affirm and those who deny, but between those who affirm and those who ignore. Listen!" he went on. "Fundamentally your mind and Amar's are similar in type; you both raise the same problems and the answers you give are the same in essence, if their substance is not the same. You advocate life's intensification, Amar its extinguishment; but you both recognise imperfection and you both aim at perfection!"

Thus it is possible to affirm or to deny the value of immediate experience as a means to spiritual development and still keep a certain spiritual integrity. But by 'those who ignore', Gokal refers to those who neglect altogether the possibilities of spiritual development which life offers; and a word or two must be said about them, for they form the necessary complement to those who seek to live their personal lives in accordance with more mature values, whose existences, however inadequate, are bound up with a desire to seek perfection. The distinction is one between the Fastidious and the Trivial, and such a distinction is fundamental in Myers's presentation.

At the beginning of the book, little Prince Jali, leaning over the balcony of the palace at Agra, had felt his heart contract with the vision of the "gigantic, heartless splendours," which the Durbar had caused to be assembled. The Emperor, present at his artificial city of Fatehpur-Sikri to receive the homage of all the Rajahs of India, is himself a visible manifestation of the spirit of materialism, of vulgarity, which marks the Empire he has raised. It is true that Akbar as an individual has his idealism and that he is not exactly happy at the way in which the influences he has let loose have manifested themselves; but to a certain extent such a perversion of his ideals is his own fault. For he is unable to conceive of any greater power than himself; according to the Din Ilahi, the new religion he has promulgated, he is to be the representative of God on earth or an equal with God: the necessarily temporal and local nature of his ideals, what might be termed his provincialism, has tainted his conceptions at their source. As the manifestations of a mind in no way remarkable, they have naturally in the course of dissemination remained true to the nature that conceived them. For, as Amar says, the Emperor is only "an average man, but raised to a higher power of manhood . . . His Majesty is the plain man, raised to a higher power." To Amar, indeed, the Emperor is a barbarian.

There is no mistaking here the 'aristocratic' basis of Myers's approval of Amar and his friends, though it is an aristocracy based on moral and spiritual principles, not social. People are not only different in outlook; throughout his work, except in *The Pool of Vishnu*, they are also different in kind. He does not deny to Akbar a kind of greatness; but that greatness is a greatness of worldliness, not of the spirit. With Akbar is associated the City of Victory, Fatehpur-Sikri, which even now is doomed, after only ten years. The irony is that of Ozymandias and of the man who built his house upon sand. Akbar is the prototype of the Great Men of all ages, the men whose conquests are merely a manifestation of their own egos, conquests which, being based on nothing more substantial than the imperfections of human personality, contain in them the seeds of their own dissolution. For Myers here, more strongly even than in *The Orissers*, sees how necessary to man is the sense of aspiration, and with it, a sense of awe towards something outside himself, provoking, in its turn, a more subtle refinement of what lies inside, and of the here and now, the immediate situation. Akbar may be of a mystical turn of mind; but it is a mysticism that is never provoked by the contemplation of anything but of the essence of himself. His Din Ilahi, a strange mixture of creeds, unexceptionable as far as it goes, is nevertheless a synthesis whose ultimate object is to exploit the personality of its founder. Hence the feeling that the India he has created (and by India, of course, we understand the modern world, the world of the 'hollow men') is unsatisfactory. It may be necessary to accept for the purpose of political manipulation the values of the court —a necessary rendering unto Caesar—but the acceptance is an essentially temporary affair, a conscious degradation to the fastidious. Not only is there the grossness and ostentation, the lack of taste, the failure of imperial society to manifest itself in forms acceptable to the discriminating; there is also the constant atmosphere of intrigue "in this land of subterranean connexions, in this land of rumours, denunciations, and blackmail." Indeed, merely as a story of political intrigue, of plot and counter-plot, where an atmosphere of tension is created, a web subtly woven, in which the various characters, whether they will or not, are inevitably enmeshed, the book is exciting and dramatic.

The people who accept the values of this world, and who, in their different ways, seek to exploit the political and social situation, receive varying degrees of sympathetic treatment. Mabun Das, lover of intrigue, ostensibly in league with Daniyal, the Emperor's younger son, but, as has been noted, secretly working for Salim, receives a measure of sympathy which is a mark of Myers's awareness that the political worldly issues are not to be regarded as negligible. At Mabun's hands, for instance, Hari is led to recognise the magnitude of what is at stake: and though a distaste for parties and factions and a realisation that he is being persuaded to attest what isn't true makes Hari a reluctant accomplice, he is forced to admit that

the disproportion between these and one's own small scruples was pretty large; one's own personal and private distaste for perjury was not an impressively weighty factor in the opposite balance.

Mabun has tact, delicacy, untiring industry; he is the "detached intelligence," consciously manipulating others for his own practical ends. Nevertheless, although he accepts Maya, the world of courts and princes, and therefore, ultimately, of illusion, he is, as Hari admits, "a man of feeling."

He rises above his own particular temperament. Never could he display a contempt for religion, parade cynicism, or ever indulge in irony.

In his concern for the Empire he contrasts favourably with Shaik Mobarek, the chief supporter of the Din Ilahi, whose Byzantine sacerdotalism based on a rigid hierarchy, then unattainable because of the irrational element, the living uncertainty, of Akbar, seeks to find its expression in Daniyal.

Ambissa, Hari's wife and Amar's sister, is the conventional ambitious woman; she accepts the values of the court in her desire to aid the fortune of her sons, for whom alone she shows any real affection.

Srilata, Amar's half-sister, unspoiled by ambition, seeks only entertain-
ment in the circles in which she moves; but this pursuit makes her indifferent to moral standards; and she "could endure a dilettantism and
triviality that positively nauseated her brother."

The sexuality underlying social relationships, a reiterated theme with
Myers, and one which, with its subtle effluences, permeates the social
scene, finds its manifestation in Lalita and Gunevati. Lalita's is a sexuality calculated to enhance her social value; she has been given "the
equipment of a courtesan, her innocence, her virginity, being reckoned
merely as an added grace." Gunevati represents a deeper animalism;
her position as Yogini to the Vamacharis, one of the mysterious underground sects to be found in India at that time, symbolises the sexuality
which is the motive force of her being, and which provides the sanction
for her every action; beyond such exploitation of her beauty she is unable to conceive any rational mode of existence. She is the human link
with that strange world of underground forces, subterranean modes of
existence which permeate Myers's description of India and from which
the rest of the characters are divided by reason or conscious effort,
whether in a worldly or spiritual direction. Gunevati is the human
being stripped of all rationality, the underlying animal which exists to
a degree in us all; and her sufferings are accepted as dumbly as those of
the cat on which Daniyal steps.

It is for Daniyal and his crew that Myers reserves his greatest distaste,
as will be shown in the analysis of the second part of *The Root and the
Flower*, *Prince Jali*. In Daniyal frivolity and triviality take on the positive
intensity of evil. For it is what Myers calls "triviality"—the word is
used frequently—which earns his deepest condemnation, rather than a
more conventional wrong-doing. His moral values and condemnation
indeed are not based on orthodox notions of right and wrong; of this
we have seen examples in *The Orissers*. Conventional 'goodness' is not
a highly prized attribute with him.

Triviality—and all those 'who ignore' are guilty of it in various
degrees—seems to Myers to have had something of the significance
which vulgarity had to Mr Failing in *The Longest Journey* and, by implication, to Mr E. M. Forster. But there are points of distinction which
will show the difference between the two artists:

Vulgarity had been the primal curse, the shoddy reticence that prevents man
opening his heart to man, the power that makes against class equality. From it
sprang all the things he hated—class shibboleths, ladies, lidies, the game laws,
the Conservative party—all the things that accent the divergencies rather than
the similarities of human nature.

Forster, it is to be noticed, regards vulgarity largely in its social setting,
in its affect on the intercourse of man to man; triviality to Myers is as

much a characteristic of the individual and springs from an inner corruption, a lack of personal taste, an inability to distinguish: "trivial
occupations" are those which have no relationship to the real business
of living, which is a constant search for ultimate truth. Amar regrets
that "trivial" matters should so preoccupy Gokal: Jali finds the people
of the Pleasance "trivial." In each case the "trivial" is implicitly contrasted with what gives significance to life, which is something that lies
beyond mere worldly intercourse. There is not so much concern for
mere fellowship in Myers as there is in Forster. Myers's attitude could
not be contained within the formula 'only connect' as easily as would
Forster's. Forster tries to bridge class distinctions, Myers, at least in the
earlier novels, accepts them; not, be it emphasised, class relationships
based on money, on property (as the world conceives them, that is to
say), but on a true community of interest, and a 'natural' affinity in
aspiration towards the ultimate and transcendental. Thus Jali, in responding to the stupidity of the Pleasance, "was merely responding
after the law of his own nature." The true aristocrat is the man whose
spiritual maturity, whose aim for perfection gives him a 'natural' transcendence, a transcendence which enables him to judge between the
trivial preoccupations of the morally vulgar and that which is significant for spiritual welfare. Thus, provided the essential quality is there,
difference of approach, as has been noted, is not so important, at least
where worldly standards are involved. By contrast, the trivial are bound
together by their inability to conceive possibilities of spiritual development. And triviality, too, involves a moral aspect which relates to conduct; expressions of triviality in behaviour automatically involve the
condemnation of those who are responsible for them. Triviality, in fact,
is Myers's version of Matthew Arnold's 'Philistinism', but associated
more with moral conduct than with cultural deficiency. With it are
connected other pejorative expressions like "frivolity," "artificiality,"
sometimes "sophistication."

Among those who do not 'ignore', to whom we must now turn, the
progress of the work brings an access in self-knowledge; there is a fuller
revelation of what underlies the assumptions behind their differing
approaches, based as these are on temperament, self-consciousness, and
a desire for perfection; a growing realisation of the need to come to
terms with the true, underlying nature of life (of which the social world
is only a distortion and in the last resort a delusion—though one to be
reckoned with) *without* sacrificing their essential fastidiousness and integrity is characteristic. In *The Near and the Far*, Hari, in *Prince Jali*, Jali,
in *Rajah Amar*, Amar move towards deeper understandings of their own
mental outlooks; they come to a realisation of themselves; and such an
understanding is, in part at least, evoked because of happenings in the

world around them. Amar appreciates the flaw in his desired abandonment of self; Jali matures through experience of self in the world of appearances; and Hari achieves reasonably satisfactory inner stability based on a more constant relationship between himself and someone outside himself. The subject of each book lies in the possibilities of spiritual living and the development of the true self for varying types of 'spiritual' temperament; the capacities of relationship between the isolated, separate individuals, weighed down in various degrees with self-consciousness and the burdens of social awareness, are explored. The individual is ultimately responsible for his own fate and must come to terms, as best he can, on the basis of his own finer awareness, with the manifestations of the outside world.

At the beginning of the first volume, Hari exists in relative unself-consciousness; unable to form out of the stuff of experience any coherent philosophy, his tendency is to greet experience as such, to live in the moment, to deny even Karma, the intuition of the moral law. Evil, which for Amar belongs to ignorance and delusion, and which will vanish "when the delusions attached to individuality have been destroyed," is part of the stuff of life for Hari. The word 'human' for him means, "fundamentally, nothing beautiful, virtuous, or intelligent, but something merely . . . strong." Life is a force to be accepted without too much seeking after fact and reason; to select is to weaken. Death must be accepted as a part of life, and the chief value of life lies in the intensity with which it is lived—whatever slavery it enjoins: better suffering, in fact, than contentment in the humdrum, especially if that suffering is a necessary concomitant of the experience of love, which for him is a supreme value. Thus he tends to seek experience as an end in itself, unrefined by deeper self-questionings. He is able to recommend to Jali: "Pretend to yourself that you are like others . . . Everyone is doing it." And he expounds his view that "Not to be afraid of this world . . . you must belong to it." These reflections are characteristic of him during his affair with Lalita. But the fact that he can consciously make such remarks reveals that there is a deeper side to his nature; he could not be aware that such conduct was possible unless he were also capable of seeing beyond it.

His relationship with Lalita is not a satisfactory one. Lalita is the affianced of Daniyal; and the secrecy imposed upon them has a wearing effect which brings to light the unsatisfactoriness of the connection. Myers reveals that for Hari at least the affair is a means to forgetfulness, for the deeper part of each remains uncommitted. Hari realises that:

Even their parting, if it came, would wear an ambiguous aspect; it would come, not because they willed it, but because they lacked the will to act otherwise.

Hari's problem, then, is one almost of adolescence: the connection with Lalita is not founded on any fundamental mutual comprehension or compatibility. Hari's uncertainty and indecision show that, despite constant assertion to the contrary, there is no genuine relationship. Other standards intrude, standards which would be irrelevant in a deeper affection, but which, based on an authority compounded of morality, common sense, expediency, and good taste, are sufficient to prove the inadequacy of their love ". . . that wretched love, which, nevertheless, had such power to torment." In other words, it is a "spiritual impotence" which affects them; and the words are significant for what Myers conceives to be a prerequisite of any genuine reciprocity. Neither can respond satisfactorily to the other because both are aware more of the external world than of each other. There is no question of conventional morality—the fact that Hari is married and Lalita betrothed does not enter into it, as is to be seen in the fact that later he accepts the love of Sita. The lack of stability, the consequent equivocation and self-deception, the inability of Hari (or of Lalita for that matter, though the affair is exposed more from his side than hers) to understand the deeper requirements of either, their mutual irresolution, provides the ultimate condemnation of their affair. As Hari, at this time, believes in nothing permanent, no emotional relationship can satisfy more than temporarily his longing for experience.

His break with Lalita only increases his restlessness. Yet he seeks, within the limits imposed by his temperament, the truth of life, as Amar notes. And those limitations have already been suggested. He can achieve no religious consummation; "in addition to the will to live a man needs must have the power to enjoy life," he considers. It is only in communion with what lies outside himself, but within the scope of the senses—aspects of the visible world—that satisfaction is to be found; and such satisfaction is necessarily temporary.

Nevertheless an intuition of peace comes to him after a conversation he has with Sita, near whom he is living, and the scene before him adds its tranquillity so that it seems to acquire a value of its own. When, however, he comes to consider the problem of behaviour, he wonders "what guidance such feelings and intuitions afford." It is the development of his love for Sita which supplies the answer and matures him as far as his nature will permit. As Sita says, his business is now to look, "not for happiness, but for something deeper out of which happiness will spring." So far he has been too wrapped up with mere zest for living; the affair with Lalita has brought about a crisis because the effort to live in the moment is seen to be insufficient.

So now begins his love for Sita. Sita, a later development of Lilian Orisser, is Amar's wife and a Christian. She follows "the sweeping simplifications of the heart" and finds beauty in the phenomenal world. This outlook of hers makes her a fitting partner for Hari. Her realisation of Amar's determination to retire from the world serves to introduce a gradual cleavage between the two which, while it never finds open expression, fills her with sadness. She cannot accept Amar's desire for withdrawal; she accepts the Western view of the intensification of life and its prolongation into eternity; it is her answer, as Gokal points out, to her realisation of human imperfection. Hence her attitude to love:

in this confused, fragmentary world love was the only power that could fuse a life into a unity and endow it with form and significance.

Hence too her demand for poetry and romance: "life without romance was, to her thinking, hardly life at all"; and hence her realisation of transience, appreciated in her chance meeting with an old crone, whose likeness she would one day herself assume, a realisation which has so often provided a theme for Western poetry.

Nevertheless, when romance is offered, at first she rejects it:

"You must love me only as you love those flowers, or as a child," she said, "or as a creature of your own imagination; but not . . . not as a woman, not as a person belonging to the real world."

And Hari, despite a feeling that a deeper relationship is possible, goes away for a time, to accompany Amar on his journey to see his dying mother.

His journey with Amar does something to reveal an alteration in Hari's nature. Momentarily, possibly under the influence of Amar's philosophical convictions, he toys with the idea of a retreat from the world. But he has too intense an awareness of the actual present. He still urges that "Life . . . gives us one hint only . . . I should say, only one command: Live!"; and he envies Amar's certainty over the presence, in the universe, of Karma, the moral law; the idea that evil always brings about its expiation is something foreign to his outlook. He regards the "true condition of blessedness" as "one in which individuality was not extinguished, but refined, intensified, and enlarged."

This idea of refinement introduces a new element which owes something to Sita. It marks Hari's subjection to a new discipline, manifested in his patience with the old Rajah Bihar, Amar's father, and his kindness in seeking Daniyal so that he may satisfy the old man's desire to entertain the prince in his house. There emerges a new moral sense which implicitly denies the attitude that life is merely there to be lived in unselfconscious and unexamined terms. He begins to appreciate certain differences of standard which are introduced by his realisation

of Daniyal's vulgarity; and his subsequent quarrel with the prince leads
to his technical imprisonment at Agra. "Daniyal and his friends happened to offend my taste," he asserts to Srilata. The development of a
sense of good taste is a new manifestation in Hari, and one which, first
hinted at in his rejection of Lalita, has been brought into greater prominence by his contact with others. Hari, in fact, is undergoing a process
of education—one might say, of civilisation—which reveals an aspect
of Myers's own mature standards and requirements for the civilised
existence. Hari still has his moments of solitariness, restlessness, and
self-dissatisfaction; nevertheless there is the beginning of a new self-
awareness, of a new maturity. The potentialities of his nature are receiving increasing attention.

The episode between Mabun Das and Hari, by bringing the two men
into explicit relationship, serves to show how Hari is aware of pro-
fundities of human existence which are beyond the pragmatic philosophy of the worldly, though not negligible, political schemer. Mabun
Das, of course, is secretly working for Salim; the accession of Daniyal
would mean the success of Mobarek's authoritarian spiritual hierarchy,
with Daniyal as Pope-Emperor; and this Mabun Das wishes to avoid.
He therefore tries to involve Hari in a plot to discredit Daniyal with his
father by proving the prince's association with the Vamachari, an
underground sect that Akbar has sworn to wipe out. Unfortunately,
Hari realises that it is not Daniyal who is involved in the sect but Salim.
He has always avoided involving himself in politics; and to this natural
reluctance is added the knowledge that to aid Mabun means commit-
ting perjury. Nevertheless he likes Mabun, appreciates his disinterest-
edness, and almost envies him his single-mindedness, his acceptance of
the socio-political world, his capacity to rest satisfied with the practical;
though at the same time he realises that Mabun is too practical:

The world is not governed by men with their definite ends, but by fate with
its unintelligible purposes. . . . If the day ever arrives when men gain control of
their worldly courses, that will be a sign that the end of the world is at hand.

For Hari has always been conscious of the power of fate, aware of the
possibilities of the unseen influences affecting men's destiny: it is a necessary corollary to his rejection of a systematic religious attitude and to
the fact that his acceptance of 'life' is more than a merely trivial swim-
ming with the stream. He therefore takes the opportunity afforded by
Gokal's illness and consequent need of him to leave Agra; and the
incident closes inconclusively. It has served to show Hari in relationship
with a complete worldling, and to reveal that he accepts standards beyond the pure exigencies of policy, even if those standards are somewhat primitive and arbitrary.

In the meantime, Sita has come to accept the growing gulf between herself and Amar. She realises the unsuitability of Hari's temporary desire for withdrawal from the world: "The world will always be real to him: he finds value in the actual moment"; she appreciates how different Amar and Hari are:

Amar was concentrated upon what was to come, and to that extent even his most unselfish actions were interested. Hari's very egotism had a disinterested quality, which it took from the fact that he was at the mercy of emotions that were not ruled by the individual will.

Hence a part of her rebels against Amar; for him wisdom is something tending away from life; for her, it is a manifestation of the poetic spirit, resting on the senses for its appreciation.

The affair of Hari and Sita draws towards its climax; Hari is the first to find stability in the new relationship. Aware that his feeling for Sita is on a different plane from that for Lalita, he puts aside all scruples with regard to Amar. For out of the flux of the external world he has found a resting place:

When he asked himself whether his present disposition was likely to be enduring, he could not see the smallest shadow of a doubt. Time might work its changes upon the substance of his love, but that love was firmly rooted, and he would carry it, for good or ill, down to the grave.

And so Hari realises the deeper implications of his own temperament; out of his joy in the real world about him experience has hewn something comparatively stable and lasting. Only Sita's reluctance for a full relationship, her desire to play with love, drives him temporarily away to Khanjo with Amar. There his love brings on a new overwhelming compassion and an understanding of his earlier narrow self-absorption; he regrets his neglect of Jali, for instance. And while he is away, Sita comes to realise the depth of her own passion, which her former life with Amar had never fully discovered. She had feared the impermanence of Hari's feeling; she realises that in the transitoriness of the sensible world, which is the obverse side of her acceptance of the poetry of existence, only love can offer any stability. And so their love, for both, takes on a deeper value, in that while both accept the worth of the moment, of experience, only the deeper reality of love can conquer the essential impermanence of that moment and of that experience. In the fulfilment of the deepest of human relationships is constancy, equilibrium, to be discovered; the love of Hari and Sita forecasts, on a slightly different basis and with a somewhat changed emphasis, the solution in terms of human relationships that Myers puts forward, in *The Pool of Vishnu*.

The Gokal-Gunevati episode is psychologically interesting, though it is not untouched by sentimentality. Gokal, a Brahmin, intellectual and friend of Hari and Amar, falls in love with Vasumati the fourteen-year-old daughter of the gardener. Vasumati dies, and her death induces a state of profound melancholy in him. For Gokal has always divided his interest between his intellectual and philosophical preoccupations and the world. His high position at court, Sita considers, must have been purchased at a certain cost to his self-esteem, for "not through intellectual eminence alone could any man, however highly gifted, hope to stand high in the world." Amar too realises that frequently Gokal's melancholy is induced by some personal mischance and deplores such a weakness; even he, however, is surprised to find how deeply Gokal grieves for the little girl. But it is not alone the girl he regrets; she merely crystallises a profounder malaise: "I am also grieving for my lost youth. I am regretting all the illusions I have not pursued, all the follies that I have not committed." He rebels against the sense of effort, that necessary willingness to reject certain types of experience to facilitate the concentration which is the prerequisite of the civilised existence. It is possible that Myers has some sympathy with his reaction; for Gokal is a character one can respect, and his romanticism is made to involve a perennial weakness of mankind. Gokal states the issue to himself:

Gokal, you are reckoned a wise man and a learned, but all that you have learned is the simplest and most ancient lesson in the world: it is better to laugh and weep like a child than to follow the wisdom of the wisest. All your life your eyes have been fastened upon the invisible; never did you look up at the fruit trees in the spring, or at the young girls blossoming around you all the year round. You have studied and pondered . . . to no profit, gaining nothing but the respect of the simple, who in reality are wiser than you.

This sentimental expression of a desire for reversion to simpler modes of being is in the last resort 'placed' by Myers. It expresses an indulgence on Gokal's part for which he finally has to pay dearly—his very disillusionment is based on an illusion.

Finally, Gokal's vision at the end of the book seems to show him certain inadequacies in Amar's search for the Absolute. The reasons given are interesting as demonstrating Myers's own approach to the question of a complete retreat from the world. For Gokal realises that the phenomenal world has a reality that makes it an essential feature of the Absolute:

"To philosophise at all," he said, "is to postulate that the process in Time calls for explanation. An explanation of it must be explicit or implicit in every system of thought, whether you call it philosophy or no."

Then he comes to see that there are shadowy forms of evil in Amar's mind . . . jealousy and suspicion; and he fears that Amar's mind "stiff-ened by logic" would be "obtuse to the awful paradoxes of the world of spirit." Amar, that is to say, has over-intellectualised his position. If he were to examine the basis of his love for Gokal, he would find that it "rests upon an intuition that a man is lovable in as much as he par-takes of the divine essence." In other words, Amar's love testifies to his unacknowledged recognition of an immanent God. Amar seeks after a delusive other-worldly purity; in his desire, based on intellect, to avoid all contact with the phenomenal world, he has mistaken his own nature. A man can only seek truth from the light within; absolute purity is impossible. The advance to the One who is Solitary is the means to grace; but the attempt to shed individuality is doomed to failure, at least in those who would base their way to release on intellect and logic.

And so Gokal turns to Gunevati, with whom he falls in love; he is the complement to Hari, for just as Hari needs to seek a permanence beyond the phenomenal world, so Gokal needs to find a sensual excite-ment in the 'real' world before he is satisfied with the effort which those who live beyond the present have to sustain.

This first book then, as will be becoming clear, is concerned with the phenomenal world in all its various aspects . . . sensuous, sensual, politi-cal, and practical; the 'near' as opposed to the 'far'. Each character prominent in this section has an awareness of inadequacy, a sense of imperfection, a dissatisfaction, a malaise. The incident at the beginning already related, of Jali and the desert, casts its shadow over the rest of the book. The Near, the approachable, the customary mode of exist-ence, is perpetually dissatisfying, even to the spiritually aware. Hari is afflicted by the inadequacy of his love for Lalita, Amar begins to ap-prehend the flaw in his desire for the extinguishment of personality; Gokal is made desolate by the emotional impoverishment of his exist-ence, Sita by the loss of her love for Amar, Jali is bewildered by the complexity of life. Underlying all the examination of personality goes a sense of flux, of restlessness, of desire for change; as one examines the deeper implications of the book, one sees the perpetual restlessness of human individuality, the realisation that a philosophy of life, an out-look on the world, must be verified by a constant groping after the deepest sources of human existence. The 'illusions' have to be explored before the treasure of the spirit is secure; it is a sign of probity that the dissatisfaction most of the characters feel leads, not to a retreat into a dead, socialised existence, but to a desire for deeper understanding. No genuine self-conscious personality, not even Amar's, can avoid the teachings of life, and by 'life' in this context is meant life as lived by self-conscious, civilised human beings willing to admit all possible imperfection, making mistakes and yet attempting to live in accordance with the deepest teachings of their experience, over against the self-satisfied artificial existence of courts and palaces, with their concessions to convention, coarseness, and hardness. Emphasising the constant un-satisfactoriness of human existence is the beautiful Indian scenery which in its tranquillity, its sense of remoteness, often takes on a colouring from the inner feeling of the character contemplating it; though it as often seems, as Hari realises, to have an independent value of its own and to offer a possible retreat, if momentary, from the preoccupations of every-day life.

The longing for retreat was an essential part of Myers's mind, as we have seen in an examination of Nicholas's character in *The Orissers*. It was one answer that he contemplated to the unsatisfactory nature of life. Something of this desire for retreat is revealed in Gokal—more still, of course, in Amar. When Gokal falls in love with Gunevati and she becomes to him, in her cheapness and stupidity, a temporary, if meretricious, solution to the effort of living, he says to Hari:

In me you find the intellectual weary of his brain-spun cobwebs; in Gunevati the child of nature, a proper toy for a second childhood such as mine . . . Before meeting her I had no idea how far I had travelled from the simple, the elementary. . . . How uninteresting is the educated mind in comparison with hers! . . . Thought crystallises into patterns of a merely formal complexity; but the instincts, with all the richness of their irrationality, belong to the creative side of life.

Animal instinct, embroidered over with the arabesques of the imagination, how can you better me that? I am tired not only of second-rate thinkers, but even of the first-rate. How many there are who think only for the sake of thinking, and what dullards they make of themselves.

A much modified version of this attitude, a modification forecast in the lightness of tone, the hint of self-mockery in Gokal's voice, comes to recommend itself to Myers in later years. The purely rational con-structions of the mind he finds dissatisfying. Though his work always had an intellectual bias, the realisation of the force of the irrational was one which, even if on intellectual grounds, he came increasingly to urge, until towards the end of his life he became strongly convinced of the evils of intellectualism. At the same time he was equally suspici-ous of irrationalism. Perhaps his best statement of his views comes in the Preface to *The Root and the Flower*; after urging a respect for moral taste, he proceeds:

Instead of calling for a sacrifice of intellectual integrity, this, as I see it, involves only a more imaginative—a more truly detached—exercise of the reason. It can hardly be doubted that the reason's most necessary task at the present time is to examine its position in the psyche as a whole, to consider under what urge it functions, within what fields it can properly legislate, what authority is should allow to mental processes other than its own, and finally what judgment to pronounce upon the rival claims—if indeed they are rival—of moral and aesthetic sensibility.

There is a distinction to be made between intellectual analysis as a technique of the author in describing his characters, and intellectual analysis as a means to reaching philosophical truth, as employed *by* the characters. In the first sense Myers remains intellectual, for he always tends to explore his characters through analysis; and he always remained more interested in philosophy than in literature. But through those characters he certainly expresses a scepticism as to the capacity of the reasoning powers to discover the ultimate truths of human existence. In *The Orissers* he recognises the deep volitions that drive human nature, suggesting that in all rational conduct there is an element of rationalisation. Amar, who is consciously intellectual, is made to realise that what he seeks is beyond the power of logic and reason to justify; as he admits to Hari, the truths of reality have to be "felt as well as heard," and prove themselves on the "immediate inward experience of the initiate." Hari, after his conversation with the Hermit on the road to Khanjo, urges explicitly that value dwells in the heart of things which the discursive reason is inadequate to discover. "For the reason was the instrument of man's conscious purposes, and these were the instruments of his unconscious purposes, and these again were but a small part of the activity of Nature or God."

Yet Gokal's adventure, as has been noted, is allowed to lead him into grave disasters; and Hari is contemptuous and Sita dismayed at the rather pathetic self-satisfaction to which Gokal's new-found theories have brought him. When Gokal is recovering from the dangerous illness which results from Gunevati's attempt on his life Hari comments on Gokal's lack of judgment:

If he continued to see the girl as she was, he never drew the practical conclusions, never anticipated the probable results in life as it went on from day to day.

Such are shown to be the practical results of disregarding too sentimentally the dictates of reason as a guide to the problem of existence. There are forms of irrationality which approach animality and invite condemnation.

In this first volume, then, in addition to the criticisms he offers of the 'worldly' characters, Myers sets out what is to be the theme of the whole book, the search for some basis of ordered life which can commend itself to a highly self-conscious individual living in the modern world. Here, through the searchings and instabilities of his characters, he begins to explore the restrictions under which the human mind works in its search for a stable existence; for all are too prone to accept the truth of 'appearances', too ready, even if they avoid the delusions of the worldlings, to be led astray by the essential flaws in their own personalities. They need to search with all their integrity before they can come to terms with the fundamental nature of life, and discover their 'real' selves behind the veils of Maya. The relationship between the sensitive individual and the various aspects of 'life'—the world of action and politics, personalities other than self, influences of the environment —is probed. The scenes of nature, the breezes that shimmer its pages, the scents and perfumes which the book exhales constantly bear witness to a consciousness of the external world; and earthly love, a genuine love based on reciprocity of feelings, is seen to be one of the highest values for those who accept the validity of experience. Intuition and experience show the vanity of seeking to avoid the burdens of individuality in the 'real' world; the phenomenal must find a place in any philosophy worthy of the name—at least for the temperaments of those who people this novel. The desire to retreat from self-consciousness, or from human contact, a desire which obviously offered its temptations, is nevertheless rejected; even thus early, Amar's point of view is shown to contain flaws which later will cause him to modify his position.

Throughout, Myers relates human actions to the metaphysical preconceptions of the characters; like Hari, he wants to know people's "underlying emotions, [their] compelling beliefs and what part they play in [their] lives." People behave as they do because they conceive of themselves as being in a certain relationship to the universe, and to the social world around them, expressed in a conscious philosophy of life. They tend to act correctly, however, in so far as they follow, not a logical system, but their being's deepest sanction. "Who is like himself?" The implications of Jali's question are becoming apparent for the work as a whole.

B. "PRINCE JALI"

The solution for Hari and Sita, with their acceptance of life and their desire for truth, has been a relationship, within the phenomenal world, of a deeper validity than anything that they have so far known. This has adduced in them a profounder stability, and a more adequate responsiveness to the possibilities of existence. For the young Jali, the achievement of stability is to be based on a knowledge of Good and Evil, on a growing experience of life, on an exploration of the social illusions as a necessary precursor to a discovery of his own real self, and on the equilibrium induced by the strength and knowledge gleaned through curiosity and the desire to understand of an adolescent youth. Evil and the great world predominate in this book, as Love and personal relationship did in the first; but with the knowledge of Evil is brought also a realisation of Good (not conventional 'goodness') based on difference and separateness of personality, recognisably to be discovered in certain individuals only—those again who refuse to ignore.

In *Prince Jali* the main features of Myers's fundamental assumptions emerge more clearly even than before. There is his aristocratism, his sense that certain lives are of greater worth than others; there is his profound moral sense and his intuitive response to certain phenomena in the universe—what, in Wordsworth's term, might be called his "feeling intellect." For in *Prince Jali* there is a surer touch, a more complete mastery of material, and a greater coherence and firmness of moral values than Myers has yet demonstrated. It is, of course, technically simpler than some of the other books, for experience is shown in its effect on a single mind and from a single standpoint—that of the little Prince. This lessens the problems of construction and permits a corresponding concentration of effect. Nevertheless, in his picture of the growing mind of the young Prince in contact with people, Myers does not neglect to relate the life of the individual to certain forces in the universe which are always thought of as existing in the background; so that experience involves at once the 'here' and the 'there', the 'near' and the 'far'. The aim is still understanding, comprehension by all powers of the mind. The effort of Jali is towards integration, an understanding which will enable him to order the centrifugal forces which he feels inside himself and which certain people about him seem to symbolise. A sureness of moral sense, based on an *intuition* of permanent values and a consciousness of superior nature, guides Jali through his various temptations. And while a part of his nature responds to these temptations, they are in the end rejected in favour of the deeper part of that very nature. The conscious intelligence strives to master, to place, to comprehend, to assimilate its intuitions by analysis and by reference to an almost instinctive standard. The ultimate effort is towards "knowledge and strength" and the confidence which they bring, as Jali himself says: a comprehension in terms of self-consciousness and self-acceptance is involved. Jali strives to bring within the scope of his conscious mind an awareness and understanding of the conduct, often irrational, of others, and to act on this understanding. It is *intelligent* (the word is frequently used in this book) in dealing with those whose motive force lies in irrationality, to assess their past and future conduct by standards which allow for this aspect of the mind. Jali, then, strives to develop a feeling intelligence.

When the book opens, we are reminded of the little Prince on the balcony at Agra at the beginning of *The Near and the Far*. There the themes had been already suggested and interrelated: the relationship, suggested by the desert, of the 'Near' and the 'Far'; the question of his own separate identity, that which makes him realise his difference from all the rest of the world; and the sense, in the killing of the snake, of those many irrational forces, largely evil, which make the world so mysterious a place—"evil in ambush." He realises that "the loneliness of being the only specimen of oneself was a part of one's own particular secret"; and at the same time "the world was undoubtedly a place of mystery and terror." The problem of *Prince Jali* is how to make this 'here' (himself) and that 'there' (the world) meet; it is the problem of experiencing and growth; like Keats, Jali can only accept the world which has been felt along the pulse, which is real to his deepest self. And his intense self-consciousness, the awareness of his separateness and of its burden which divides him even from his parents, is made the worse by his desire for secrecy, and his fear of the world. Only one thing sustains him and provides him with a possible guide in the midst of so manifold and great dangers; what at first seems to him a handicap but what later he sees as his greatest strength—his sense of his own nature, nurtured in the civilised environment of his father's court. He had in fact grown up

in a community where tradition survived, where manners were still in their golden age, and hardness, coarseness, and ostentation had not yet taken root.

On this what Myers frequently terms Jali's "fastidiousness," his "*natural* taste," is based; from this standpoint Jali judges harshly those in the palace around him.

Yet there is as yet no certainty, no maturity in his outlook. The search is for a true basis of strength through understanding; the deeper implications of that moral superiority implied in the quotations above have to be demonstrated; this provides an opportunity for more of the 'illusions' to be explored and 'placed'.

For, at first, this very fastidiousness provides Jali's chief stumbling-block. His sense of difference from those around him makes him blame, not the world, but himself. He must assume an outward shape, as he sees others doing, which will satisfy those he comes into contact with, and make him recognisable in their terms. By doing this he will shake off his fears and be able to connect with others, thus shedding some of the burden of separateness. He must amalgamate with the world, not yet realising "that refinement is the hardest thing in the world to dissimulate." And so he accepts the world of appearances, for it was "appearances that formed the bridge between person and person";

people, he considers, had "to choose between *seeing* and *being*." Moreover, as by a further subtlety of thought he realises later, illusion as illusion has to be explained: "things were not imagined, that is to say, invented, or created without there being some reason behind it," and Jali rejects his father's mere "intellectual constructions" because Kali—what Gunevati stands for—is at least as real as Amar's abstract ideas.

Jali *sees* everything, but *is* nothing—for he has no success in his relations with others, and therefore achieves no identity in their minds. And so he attempts to offer something graspable which will make them appreciate his presence; he offers a social identity by which the worldlings will recognise him as one of themselves. All the time, however, he is held back from full connivance with the society around him by the feeling of his own identity, an identity which seeks knowledge and understanding, but of such a sort as will tally with inner feeling and intuition. It must square with his own sense of the reality of evil—an apprehension which makes him reject Buddhism, for instance. His problem—and Myers's own incidentally—is conveyed in his appreciation that "the true self seemed to be isolated by its own inalienable nature from other true selves."

The first stage in his probings into the question of identity is marked by his relationship with Gunevati, involving a temporary acceptance of one aspect of social illusion, which yet seems to have, for the moment, a greater reality than the paradoxical 'nothingness' of himself.

Gunevati displays an "animal serenity;" Myers makes it plain that she is to be considered on a lower material plane than Jali, but for the moment she is to the prince simply one who "could establish contact with anyone in the world." She is "splendidly irrational . . . No principles of any abstract ethic, no needfulness of self-government, did she know." This is significant in view of the end to which Gunevati comes. Myers, as we have noted, will sanction intuition, but not sheer animal irrationality. Gunevati represents sex—her incarnation as the Goddess of the Vachamari is symbolic of her position. In her teachings Jali finds "a belief that he had discovered the necessary bond between himself and society." Her simplified vision gives him a temporary admittance to society because, by making plain to him certain of the motive forces behind human kind, she permits him to assume a temporary personality in terms of those forces. And so for a time he becomes a young rake. Gunevati's ideas on sex are grounded on the actual observable behaviour of human beings. For a moment, then, his fastidiousness lapses; he doubts the superiority of any one system of thought to another. Each one lives in a world of his own: who will say one is superior to the other?

But gradually Jali comes to see the inadequacy of Gunevati, at least for himself. If he can, for a moment, see the world as she sees it, and follow her tuition—a course of conduct in which he is successful—

he was quite unable to *feel* and accept the world as she felt it and accepted it: that, he saw, would never be within his power. Her temperament was what it was because she had no other self behind; but, when he adopted her vision, he did it of set intent, and his own self lay behind, remaining absolutely unchanged.

And not only is there his innate self to challenge her and his own new mode of life; there is the standard set by his parents and their inborn tastes, "their distaste for sensuality, their dislike of unreason and disorder." He cannot fundamentally accept Gunevati's lack of moral taste. Once more, then, he realises his uniqueness; he feels for his lost innocence; the *effect* of upbringing and early environment cannot be wiped out. The intuition of Karma, the moral law, already exists: Gunevati is judged by a higher standard than she represents. A crisis comes when Jali is taken by his mother to the Christian chapel at Fatehpur-Sikri. He faints, and on recovering, the impulse to confess his relationship with the girl becomes strong; but he resists because the sense of his own isolation yet exists still more strongly. He must fight his own battles, for he realises that the desire to be good can be more demoralising than the desire to be wicked:

The longing for goodness and purity had its reverse side, which was a longing for relief from responsibilities, effort, and danger. One had one's self-respect to consider.

And this introduces us to another aspect of his character and another side of the conception of selfhood, identity, personality. Identity may bring with it fear and pain and suffering, a desire to sink back into community with others, to become one of the mob; but it is also a means to a higher idea of self-respect, to a fuller realisation of the potentialities of being on the protestant basis of determination and truth to self, or self-effort leading to self-knowledge. In any case, Jali realises it is not possible to go back; confession under these circumstances would seem a self-betrayal, a desire for a removal of responsibility. Affection for parents is in Jali's present state a weakness, because, though he realises what they stand for, as an order, a way of life, that order is not yet *his* order; it exists merely as a possible standard—one which in his better moments he can accept—among others. Understanding (as in Keats) must precede acceptance: the 'here' and the 'there' must coalesce. Jali senses, too, something unsatisfactory about his parents; they have, perhaps, the "unconscious will to ignore"; they do not see much that goes on as clearly as he does. Thus, though his parents provide him with a standard, that standard is not itself immune from criticism.

Hence his relationship with Gunevati is not yet abandoned; now, however, she begins to affect him as something evil, whereas before she had merely offended his taste. As his knowledge increases, so does his grasp over the relative values of the mysterious world in which he finds himself. Her value to him now is not so much sexual; she becomes a source of secret knowledge, a key, unconscious perhaps, to certain aspects of life that he must discover if he is to make an assured judgment on a basis of knowledge. She represents the underground stirrings of passion "half-religious, half-erotic, which dominated the spirit of the race"; and these he wishes to learn about, for he lives less in his senses than in his thinking and enquiring mind. Gunevati's connection with the people of the Valley where Jali is staying at Khanjo with his mother interests him. His growing sense of her evil is indicated by his appreciation of her relations with Mujatta, the herb-woman, who exercises so corrupting an influence over the natives, and with the people of the valley. The Valley itself seems to partake of the evil of her presence. Kali takes on many shapes—even that of the world around him:

He could not endure these confining mountain slopes muffled in sombre trees, the meagre sky-space, the absence of horizon. The people of the valley, too, were filled with the dull, instinctive malevolence of an inferior race.

The incident of the bear-cub confirms this instinctive reaction against his environment at Khanjo permeated with the influences of Gunevati and her friends, devotees of Kali, symbol of disorder. For these are the people with whom she stands in "instinctive sympathy," perhaps in "secret alliance."

But Jali also begins to perceive that she has contacts with the great world; she is playing a part, obscure but influential, in the affairs of Empire. It is the gradual unfolding of this fact which gives an added depth and significance to the book. Jali and his adventure are not isolated from the affairs of imperial life; if there is a perception of dark mysterious spiritual influences at work, the more mundane affairs of the political life of India, with their sinister connections and interrelations are kept constantly before our minds. Gunevati comes to be invested with a political as well as a 'spiritual' significance. And if Myers's and Jali's interest is primarily in the latter, the former is not forgotten; it provides as we shall see, the climax to the book. The disorderly, unhealthy society of India is aptly symbolised by its cruelty to Gunevati in the removal of her tongue.

Gunevati, then, is associated with the world outside—the world of "dissensions, intrigues, and murders." Hence her discontent and her hatred of Gokal, who would keep her from the excitements of the greater world. (Hence, too, she forms a link between Mujatta of the Valley and Daniyal and the Pleasance; Gunevati becomes the symbol of those who 'ignore' in their various modes of spiritual blindness, and so she provides a connection between one setting of evil and the next.) Jali has now arrived at a deeper comprehension of Gunevati in all her irrationality. This enables him to understand her, while his parents, despite their greater moral fineness, are blind. Common sense, he realises, is out of place in dealing with her:

Gunevati was a creature of impulse, mixed with cunning. Her calculations, starting from irrational premises, would work to irrational conclusions.

And so he realises that, in alliance with Mujatta, she will attempt to kill Gokal. There follows a long episode in which he strives to circumvent her schemes—though the forces allied against him are too strong. The story is told with considerable power and intensity as the uncertainties in the situation mount up. For Jali's understanding, though right in the main, has still some gaps. Mujatta remains something of an unknown quantity; and it is in the end the intervention of unknown quantities— Salim's people—that defeats him. Only the old cook and he have real- ised that Gokal has brought evil into the valley with him; and Gokal has to pay, nearly, with his life.

The responsibility, once the poisoning has occurred, is removed from Jali's hands. Gunevati flees and, with the partial recovery of Gokal, the evil seems to be lifting. Moreover, he and Sita are to join his father at Ravi, which means that the hated valley is left behind. As they reach open country, his sense of escape becomes complete; and he is carried away with transports of joy. Gokal is recovering; and Jali feels that the past is done with, little realising what is in store.

At Ravi, his first contact is with Ali, Hari's son. Ali, whom he had known at Agra as a good-looking young man fond only of sports, now betrays all the attributes of a man of the world, displaying a familiarity (but as it turns out, only of the most superficial nature) with books, pictures, and music. Jali is to be introduced to the Arts.

By the Arts, however, is not implied a deep concern for the moral values which they can reveal, but a shallow and petty aestheticism. Daniyal, at whose Pleasance Ali is residing, is "the Poet, the Artist, the enraptured lover of Beauty." The ironic intent emerges in the capitals. The shallow sophistication of the Camp, triviality in another of its mani- festations, recalling Comus and his crew, earns Myers's condemnation. He was himself not deeply interested in modern literary or artistic crea- tion, perhaps because he saw the shallower side of what is all too fre- quently only a coterie movement—a means of self-gratification and self-indulgence leading to a pitiable type of self-satisfaction.[1] The Camp provides an example of this; it glories in its independence of thought, its freedom from convention, its glorious emancipation from the Philistine and the Prig. It casts off "dreary actuality." Here, everybody is somebody—in his own estimation; "in artificiality the spirit finds its true life"; revolt is the order of the day, revolt against the old outworn conventions, prejudices, and "above all, the bullying, nagging disposition of nature." But, as Myers shows, and as Jali comes to realise, the camp "had its own inverted orthodoxy."

The Camp taught that thinking for oneself consisted in nothing more than in reversing established opinions, that the newest thing was necessarily superior to one that came before and that the ultimate test of the worth of an idea was its capacity to startle the Philistine and annoy him. They depended basically upon a solid, shockable world of decorum and common sense.

Myers, in *The Orissers*, has already given his opinion of fashion—the desire for novelty at any cost. Here, in a deeper analysis, he connects fashion with a literary and artistic pretentiousness which, far from having any real independence, relies on the background of respectable people to shock and thus to provide it with its *raison d'être*. For, as he acutely notices, without that background, the Arts as Daniyal sees them would lack any interest.

The pettiness of this outlook is admirably illustrated in the Camp's absurd attitude to nature and naturalness. The dead trees, artificially raised on the planking on which the Pleasance stands, the leaves attached to the twigs by wire, the doves dipped in gold or silver paint, the ostentatious baroque architecture in all its gaudy splendour, point to the absurdity and pretentious artificiality of the spirit animating such a structure. The gossip, the homosexuality, the petty sense of conflict for favours, the inverted conventionality ("To each the voice of fashion was absolutely peremptory: what fashion enjoined, that they were eager to accept, repeat, believe, and practise, without even a thought of dissent") are signs, not of sin, which at least might prove the inhabitants

---

[1] Cf. p. 143. Myers's analysis bears an interesting relationship to Henry James's very similar assessment of Gilbert Osmond in *The Portrait of a Lady*: ". . . under the guise of caring only for intrinsic values Osmond lived exclusively for the world. Far from being its master as he pretended to be, he was its very humble servant, and the degree of its attention was his only measure of success. He lived with his eye on it from morning till night, and the world was so stupid it never suspected the trick. Everything he did was *pose*—*pose* so subtly considered that if one were not on the lookout one mistook it for impulse. Ralph had never met a man who lived so much in the land of consideration. His tastes, his studies, his accomplishments, his collections, were all for a purpose. His life on his hill-top at Florence had been the conscious attitude of years. His solitude, his ennui, his love for his daughter, his good manners, his bad manners, were so many features of a mental image constantly present to him as a model of impertinence and mystification. His ambition was not to please the world, but to please himself by exciting the world's curiosity and then declining to satisfy it."

to be men of character, but of "small self-conscious immoralities."
Spectacular villainies, vileness on a great scale might have been more
comprehensible; but Gunevati, when telling of her love for Daniyal,
can reveal only "meannesses, trickeries, and deceits, all of a most con-
temptible pettiness."

At first, Jali accepts this glittering, meretricious world; and when he
sees through Ali, he still thinks that the Prince must somehow be different. Disillusionment soon follows; Daniyal's play reveals the true
character of its author, and finally disillusions Jali as to the worth of the
Camp:

> For the first time in his [Jali's] life it was being given to him to view the full
> breadth of the gulf by which our human nature can be sundered in its estimate
> of what is pleasant and admirable in this world.

It is interesting to note that Myers makes this disillusionment quite ingenuous—based not on conscious literary canons but on *natural* moral
taste combined with a growing experience: Jali "was merely responding after the law of his own nature."

Ravi now becomes as sombre as Khanjo. The standard represented by
his parents comes increasingly to Jali's mind; it is something to cling to:

> His love, his true respect, for the human beings on this side of the lake seemed
> to him to offer something trustworthy and admirable amidst all the shifting
> sands of the world.

Only curiosity, the desire to learn, to know "by what law had [all these]
come together" leads him still to visit the Camp. "Certainly if a man
were to lose his curiosity he would very soon fade away into death."
He realises that Gunevati and these people are monstrous—but they are
interesting, fascinating almost, with a sort of interest that his own
people, those "governed by moral fastidiousness, by sensitiveness, by
generosity," lack. People, he has learnt, are not naturally guided by
"reason and goodwill."

He is seized once more with a desire to confess to his people; for he
comes to suspect that Gunevati's appearance at the Camp has important
political implications; the question of responsibility in fact arises, his
responsibility for the safety of Hari and Gokal, whom Gunevati by an
over-indulgence in gossip might well ruin. But he goes on to consider,
as before, that his friends and parents live in a fictitious world; in a way,
therefore, he considers, they have really only themselves to blame for
anything that may happen. So he still avoids confession:

> Safety and goodness lay over there [with his people]. But he could not, it
> seemed, embrace the good singleheartedly—no, not yet! He must first taste
> other experiences, so that, when he did reject the world, it should be with the

disdain bred of complete knowledge and competence. Before embracing the good, he must be assured he was doing it out of knowledge and strength.

Nevertheless, the Camp seems to him increasingly detestable. Moreover, he comes to see that all this world, from Ambissa to Gunevati, from Daniyal to Jagashri Ranee, is somehow bound together. These people represent, in multiplicity, a unified attitude towards life; they are spiritually akin, in that the social world provides their standards.

One of the elements in the situation is Gunevati's love for Daniyal. It is possible that this love, which Daniyal fails to return, will lead her, in an effort to attract the Prince, to indiscretions. Jali therefore watches her closely, and becomes aware of her profound worldly significance. The evil in her is no disease, not the result of hysteria or nerves—no psychopathological explanation is possible. Instead

she was overawed by the ruthlessness of the forces by which she was carried along. In operation those forces were enormous and implacable; in essence they were trivial, haphazard, and unworthy of respect.

Also

Her perversity and triviality were as stubborn and fateful as any of the virtues of wise and saintly men . . . while she stood for so little in herself, she represented so much in the world.

Jali now attempts to find out how much Gunevati has already revealed. Then comes the climax of the episode, the cutting out of Gunevati's tongue, which concentrates in one appalling action the essence of the book. It is the judgment of the world on the worldly; those who live by its standards expose themselves to its punishments; it is the sign of Gunevati's temporal importance; it demonstrates the implacable forces with which Gunevati is associated and which turn against her; it epitomises the evil so frequently hinted at in the book; and by its concreteness it drives all these things home in the way only a novel makes possible.

In the meantime Jali, realising that Hari will himself tell all, decides to confess about his relationship to Gunevati; not only because to be found out is now inevitable, but because by doing so he is cleaving to those with whom he has a true communion. Only one thing he regrets —his difficulty in expressing his full sense of the detestableness of the Camp. He realises that it represents evil—it is not just negatively bad, but, representing what it does in the world, positively hateful. (It is to be noted that Myers's attitude has developed from the rather petulant attitude of Nicholas to Jali's full-blooded condemnation.)

His open-mindedness had vanished completely; he now knew that he hated Daniyal and his company with a hatred so violent that it would listen to no arguments on the other side. His rage against his father and Hari sprang from the knowledge that he would be unable to kindle in them a flame of hatred equal to his own. . . . His secret desire was to make use of his father and others as instruments of his vengeance, to set upon Daniyal like a host of avenging furies.

It is a comment on the weakness of the "nice people" that the avenging furies are only able to make Rajah Amar's futile gesture of hatred against Daniyal at the end of *Rajah Amar*. But the fact of the condemnation is unequivocal. So much life has taught Jali; understanding, curiosity are not sufficient. There must also be acceptance and rejection with all the force of being, emotional as well as intellectual.

Nevertheless, though Jali's confession binds him to his own people, is an act bringing him into integral contact with those who matter, the sense of isolation still haunts him:

To explain the bare facts of the case would be possible no doubt, but bare facts were often misleading; and when it came to communicating subtle shades of feeling, conjecture, and intuition, how hopeless the undertaking appeared!

Jali still has his feeling of spiritual aloneness, a fact which is demonstrated in another outburst against the "nice people" and their stupidity in not seeing things as he sees them; he at least, he considers, is aware of his own stupidity. The difficulties of contact—a perpetual theme with Myers—are not resolved in this volume. And so in a way the novel closes inconclusively—with Jali's equivocal sense of isolation-in-community:

In his mind there was no sunlight; the darkness of the night still remained there—a darkness that was not of that night only, but of the whole long night of humanity's suffering and evil-doing.

Evil has been understood and spiritual rottenness revealed; but what hope has the individual to affect forces so implacable and deep, when even his allies are uncertain? The answer does not come unequivocally until Jali's education is completed in *The Pool of Vishnu*. Nevertheless, one thing is certain—even if these people of the Pleasance express only their own natures, moral health demands their destruction.

Many writers, since about the middle of the last century, have written about childhood. Although Jali is still a young boy, the book contains little of the child's peculiar response to the external world. Curiosity is there, provides indeed the motive force for much of Jali's conduct; but it is a curiosity that attaches itself not to things in the sensible world but to the behaviour of people. Even allowing for the comparative maturity of the Eastern as opposed to the Western child, Jali seeks a type of knowledge that is the concern of late adolescence and early manhood, rather than childhood. The sense of personal identity which comes with puberty is the starting point for his investigations, but one feels on occasions that the peculiar social susceptibilities are the impositions of an older mind—or at least that the analysis to which they are subjected (for children are socially extraordinarily aware in an almost subconscious way) emerges from the ruminations of later experience.

The book, then, is not a particularly successful picture of typical childhood. But in fact it is not intended to be so except in so far as it delineates a child peculiarly precocious in moral sense and wishing to know the fact and reason of others in a particularly intellectualised sort of way in order to feel at home in the world. As a description of an early attempt to achieve integrity in this sort of way, unusual but by no means impossible, it succeeds admirably. Certainly its subject is 'growing up'; it conveys excellently if in a somewhat telescoped fashion the response of a particular kind of adolescent mind to the circumstances of existence. If the 'smell' of life is lacking, the growth of mental experience—a perfectly proper subject for a novelist—is admirably conveyed through fact and incident; and the growing boy's mental gropings after comprehension emerge from and in their turn coalesce with the incidents of the book. In other words, the continuity of experience expressed in the concrete happenings of this section is adequately related to the growth in mental and moral stature which is the real theme of the novel. Jali's development at the end is not complete; there is adolescent rejection of the meretricious based on an understanding that yet lacks a full growth of human sympathy. But that understanding has reached a certain stage which, if it has not learnt to forgive its enemies, has yet found how to separate the sheep from the goats. Jali has come to a realisation of Good and Evil, if not of good-and-evil. That in itself is a considerable achievement which in some ways his author never got beyond, though he attempts to do so in *The Pool of Vishnu*. To tell the *whole* story from the point of view of the boy was perhaps an artistic mistake; for it never allows Myers to see the problem of growth in all its complexity, as for instance George Eliot was able to do in *The Mill on the Floss*. And Jali's reaction of *hatred* to the Pleasance, representing as it did the attitude of his author, remains perhaps adolescent. One senses, indeed, personal overtones symptomatic of Myers's own attitude. For the moment, however, Jali must be left in the security of his advance in awareness; his father is the main subject of the next book.

C. "RAJAH AMAR"

Rajah Amar had been an important character in the other two novels: here he comes to the centre. But already we have been introduced to the problem that Amar represents. It is a problem which interested

Myers deeply and one which played a vital and important part in his own life.

Amar, as we have seen, forms one of that group of highly sophisticated and self-conscious beings whose questionings and probings into the world of 'being' cause them to stand over against the 'world'. Although in certain ways he respects Akbar, he nevertheless feels superior to him. "His [Amar's] pride was rooted in ideas of racial, cultural, and intellectual superiority," we remember. A Buddhist by intellectual conviction, he aims to put into practice the Buddhist doctrines, and these he has discovered in their original purity as a result of research into the real significance of Gautama's word.

At first Amar condemns the Mahayana as a whole, for "by shifting the emphasis from self-discipline to altruism" it had falsified the original Buddhist conception:

No man could help his fellow save by the force of his example, save by the spectacle of his achieved wholeness.

Amar, then, seeks to withdraw from the world, and to shake off the bonds of individuality, identity, selfhood, which he conceives to be the ultimate illusions. He rejects the idea of a personal God, in fact, and seeks an Absolute that is only attainable through a self-discipline which removes him from 'personality', and such illusions as surround the flesh. He has already devoted some years to his meditations and has reached a comparatively advanced stage, so that at the beginning of the book that bears his name he can contemplate retirement from the world in a matter of weeks.

Nevertheless, Amar is also a ruler; and in view of the conflict that seems likely to break out between Daniyal and Salim for the succession to the throne of Akbar it is necessary for him to take a stand on one side or another so that he can leave a reasonably clear-cut policy for Sita and Gokal to follow when he hands over the reigns of government to them as regents for his son, Jali. The contemplative as politician, then, is one aspect of the drama of Amar. But even more interesting is the way in which the decision to withdraw from the world is shown to be based on false premises, and the flaw in Amar's integrity revealed. It is a flaw the nature of which he is gradually brought to realise through the course of events and the fundamental honesty of his own nature. The case of Amar is in fact a fundamental case for Myers himself; Amar is a grown-up Nicholas, wiser, more poised because his creator has himself moved towards a solution of the problem that Nicholas evoked; Amar is more self-consistent and exposes deeper levels of human nature than did Nicholas. There is much of Myers himself in Amar, as Mrs Myers has pointed out to me.

First, it is necessary to examine the way in which Amar approaches the problems of rulership in the earlier books. Despite his growing aloofness from the world, Amar is presented as a man of deep experience who has acquired a natural distaste for the material mode of life and has reacted against the spiritual vulgarity which mars the existence of the court:

> Sita would see him leading a way of life that was distasteful to him and cultivating a society that he despised.

Nevertheless at first he sees the necessity of fighting the world with its own weapons; to do so, he needs to accept certain of the postulates of the world. Such an acceptance, he thinks, can stand apart from his self-avowed resolve to retire. He tries, therefore, to create a division between expediency and ultimate moral values. "Render unto Caesar . . ." is the aphorism that best represents his attitude. In this he is contrasted with his wife, Sita, who, though a Christian, is not convinced of the wisdom of such a policy. She believes that no such dichotomy is possible and she is unable to detach policies from personalities, as her husband attempts to do. Her belief in Christianity induces in her a belief in the phenomenal world and in right action, as we have seen.

> For his [Amar's] part he found little difficulty in sifting out questions of personality from questions of policy, but Sita was otherwise constructed.

Amar has a mind that moves towards abstraction and logic; his idea that "right behaviour is not an end in itself but merely one of the conditions that a man must satisfy in order to reach his goal," makes him naturally less interested in personality and he regards the policy as an abstract conception that can be imposed regardless of those who have to put it into practice. As he says to Hari "the choice between Salim and Daniyal is a political one. I am not interested in Daniyal's private affairs." Amar's idea was one that Myers himself was coming to reject, and the results of his rejection we shall see more fully in *The Pool of Vishnu*. For the moment it is only necessary to point to the failure of Amar's attitude as an indication of the way in which the mind of his creator is moving.

Amar, however, is fully capable of assessing people at their worth. One of the features of his character is that moral fastidiousness which Myers himself so amply possessed; and although Amar favours the party of Daniyal, he has little difficulty in summing up the true worth of the prince. The relative values of the two characters are clear to Hari when Daniyal visits Amar at Ravi:

> But contact with Amar's mind (even of this gingerly sort) had the effect of concentrating Hari's attention upon the vulgarity of Daniyal. His sense of it in

the past had remained floating in suspension; a drop of acid from Amar's particular fastidiousness had been needed to precipitate it.

Not that Amar was himself wholly conscious of his own attitude or whence it came:

Amar's standards were so completely a part of his heritage that he was never really conscious in his application of them.

He despises the prince with a "well satisfied disdain." This, perhaps, points to one of his weaknesses. For Amar in certain respects is egotistical, and his aloofness is not always a very attractive trait. His *desire* for Nirvana is undoubtedly strong. The appeal of peace, tranquillity, repose, is considerable. As Amar contemplates the lake by his house on one occasion he considers:

some day it would surely be granted him to identify himself with this repose, and to exist, selfless, brooding upon the face of these serene waters,

and on another he contemplates the mountain tops with a keen desire to rise above them into the rarified tranquillity that they represent. But he finds it difficult to abstract himself from earthly things. There is his fondness for Jali and, intermittently, his feeling for Sita. There is his apprehension of the phenomenal world—even a sharp horse-ride makes him realise what he will lose. The failure of Daniyal to visit his father at Ravi and his subsequent resentment that the old man should be disappointed make him understand that his throwing off of the bonds of selfhood is less complete than he had thought. Nevertheless these are only incidentals, pointers. The error into which he is falling has more important repercussions than these.

Hari first warns him of a deeper, more philosophical flaw in his determination.

Your mind is too reasonable for me, and believing, as I do, that reason itself is delusive, I prefer to take my delusions from nearer to their source,

is Hari's way of putting it. And later Gokal realises that Amar's mind is too "stiffened by logic" to be able to understand "the awful paradoxes of the world of spirit." Both Hari and Gokal accept the idea that an adequate philosophy must be one that explains the phenomenon of life-in-time. Hari's attitude admittedly is not satisfactory; and though he is able to point to an important lack in Amar's outlook, Hari's own positive hedonistic view ("Life . . . gives us one hint only . . . Live!") is not adequate. Nevertheless Hari indicates certain depths and reaches of personality that Amar has ignored—and ignored, as we see later, to his cost.

I think it is you who are the rebel, Amar; and a more desperate one than I, for what you are rebelling against in yourself is more powerful than either reason or morality.

As Hari has earlier realised,

how can a man, enclosing himself in the solitude of his own self-conscious will, win freedom from the differentiation of personality. . . . Is he not following a road that will carry him farther and farther into the inward maze and tighten the knot of self-hood?

It becomes even more clear, through the account of Gokal's vision at Ravi, that Amar has chosen the wrong road. Gokal realises "the reality and significance of the phenomenal world as a feature of the Absolute" as against Amar's conception that the Absolute is "simply that of which nothing could be predicted." Amar has tried to reach his Absolute by reason and logic; he has sought to crush certain of his intuitions and emotions and by so doing has left in his mind "jealousy and suspicion and other shadowy forms of evil." In other words, Amar's austerity has led him to ignore certain parts of the mind that will not be crushed as easily as he had hoped and which in the subconscious will yet exact a penalty. He has used his intelligence instead of his instinctive apprehension and thus has failed in self-knowledge. In the fantasy of his vision Gokal uses Amar's love for him to try to show Amar the error of his outlook. Amar loves Gokal because they are brothers in aspiration; and that love, as Gokal says,

rests upon an intuition that man is lovable in-as-much as he partakes of the divine essence. You will see that your love addresses itself to the divine. Such love is in you and it testifies to your unacknowledged recognition of God.

In the vision, Amar denies this: he admits that love is the last of the imperfections to fade away, but nevertheless, he takes his stand "upon the wisdom of the Enlightened One."

The vision of Gokal brings to a head, in a symbolic manner, the real problem of Amar. The riddle there posed has to be solved in real life by Amar himself; and what in the vision exists on a high philosophical transcendental plane is worked out in worldly terms in *Rajah Amar*. The book tells of Amar's incursion into the political world and his failure to put into practice the political scheme of action that had been foreshadowed in the earlier book. He has decided, it will be remembered, to support Daniyal in spite of his personal distaste for the prince. He is to find that the rejection on intuitive grounds is a surer basis for action than a self-conscious rational attempt to distinguish personalities and policies.

Myers gives us a description of Amar in the introduction to this last part of the trilogy. The greater part of the book is written in the form of Amar's diary and several rather tedious devices are employed to give a certain appearance of genuineness to the document; but before the diary is revealed, Myers affords us a useful hint as to the nature of the supposed writer. He is a "highly self-conscious and self-critical gentleman" with a taste for a neat irony; and the journal is described as the revelation of a spirit "serious and sincere" who, though not of the world and certainly not *for* the world, yet endeavours to render "gratefully and in exact measure unto Caesar the things that are Caesar's." This introduction gives us an indication of Myers's capacity for detachment. The Rajah is a highly self-conscious, fastidiously poised character like himself. But Myers is able to preserve the necessary distance from his own creation, to see round him as it were, and place him in a proper perspective.

The whole of the story is woven round Amar and Daniyal; though Daniyal does not actually appear until the end of the book, he is never long absent from our minds. At the beginning Amar is brought up against Mobarek, who hopes to use Daniyal in his scheme for settlement of the Empire along hierarchical lines. Mobarek's dominant characteristic is, as Amar notes,

a passion for organisation, and for the discipline that organisation both requires and enforces. I respect this trait. In the individual it betokens self-respect and in the race it makes for civilisation.

Yet the Rajah is critical of the Shaik. Mobarek is too concerned with grading human beings, "and the standard he uses is not a good one." Transcendental values are not accepted as supreme: "they are given a place on a scale that is essentially worldly . . . From first to last he is incapable of disloyalty to the caste spirit." Mobarek in fact, views human beings, not according to spiritual worth, but in deference to birth and other purely conventional and worldly standards. Thus Mobarek stands for 'civilisation' in a sense that Myers increasingly dislikes; and Amar is expressing something of his creator's own feeling when he states:

If a civilised community be defined as one where you find aesthetic preoccupations, subtle thought, and polished intercourse, is civilisation necessarily desirable? Aesthetic preoccupations are not inconsistent with a wholly inadequate conception of the range and power of art; thought may be subtle and yet trivial; and polished intercourse may be singularly uninteresting.

Thus, although Amar remains socially conservative, he yet rejects Mobarek's caste system. He seeks no revolutionary changes; indeed, he explicitly reproves disrespect for superiors in a way which contrasts interestingly with his creator's later views:

To be without respect, or to pretend to be without respect, for those who stand high above you—this is to be guilty of either an unintentional or an intentional stupidity,

and later, in reaction against Daniyal, Amar comments:

A group of conscientious, energetic, and for the most part able men, engaged upon the thankless and difficult task of government, Daniyal sees—or pretends to see—as a collection of stupid, cruel, and ridiculous scoundrels.

If there is an occasional air of priggishness about Amar, he is not unaware of this fault in himself. "I wanted to show Mobarek that I was not afraid of being a prig." A further meeting with Daniyal enables Amar to castigate the "Art of creating social appearances" when nothing matters "except that there should be the requisite amount of noise and laughter"; and the Rajah's comment is expressive of the man: "This business of acting up to an agreed standard of elegance is to my mind a very tiresome business." The dislike that Amar shares with his author for any form of exhibitionism is clearly brought out; at the Camp he senses "a naturalness too good to be true, an exaggerated *sans-gêne*, a daring which pretends to be unaware of itself."

Indeed Amar's character is revealed in a number of deft touches; the austere nature of his manner, with its honesty of purpose and clear-sightedness, is built up convincingly. "I am," he observes, "an exceptionally unsuitable object for the exercise of charm"; and his dry comment to the effect that the words of Churaman (one of the court officials) "were spoken in that candid and confidential tone of voice that at once inspires mistrust" gives a clear insight into the detached and critical observer. He admits himself to be lacking in geniality—on the grounds that to be genial means not only to overlook other people's shortcomings but, more important, one's own.

But for the moment Amar gets on fairly well with Mobarek and accepts the Shaik's offer to ride with him to meet the Khan and Lalita, who are on their way to join Daniyal at Kathiapur. *En route*, by a chance that perhaps fails to convince, they encounter Smith, the humanist philosopher from the West, who at that time is studying the religious thought of the East, and travelling across India to do so. The discussion with Smith, who is on his way to join Daniyal, brings out certain features of Myers's own thought on the question of humanism. Already he had expressed something of his attitude in *The Orissers*. This episode enables Myers to reinforce his earlier opinion that humanism is an emasculated philosophy. It tends to emphasise the 'literary' nature of the book in its self-conscious attempt to introduce an outlook on life for the purpose of discussion and dissection, something rather too overtly apart from the demands of plot and incident: imposed on the structure of the book rather than growing inevitably out of it.

Smith is an academic type bearing a considerable likeness, in outlook, to Lowes Dickinson; Myers's objection—an objection, of course,
he voices through Amar—to Smith's intellectual position, with its
emphasis on the Greek view of life, is based on his conception of the
inadequacy of the Greek point of view. To Smith, the fact that the
Greeks had made people feel at home in the world and had succeeded
in banishing certain religious ideas—he calls them "terrors" and "superstition"—was a mark of their superiority to other races. He admires the
rationality of the Greek conception. This view of existence fails to satisfy Amar. "The Greeks," he says, "had a lively intellectual curiosity,
but little capacity for wonder or adoration," and later:

The Greek liked to think of himself as a member of a city community, but
his city was, none the less, a point upon the wandering earth, and the earth is a
point in the universe and every part of the universe partakes of the metaphysical
mystery of its being.

In other words, what Smith sees as the primary achievement of the
Greeks, their banishment of mystery from man, Amar regards as their
greatest failing. Life, as Myers always believed, must be transcendent-
ally sanctioned. The Greeks believed the only means of discovering the
truth about the world was through the reasoning mind of man; whereas, much better,

the Jew addressed himself to men's intuitions and spoke in the language of
inspiration. It is this that has given Christ's utterances their unexampled power.

And so, in his lack of understanding of the moral and spiritual order
of the universe, Smith is shown as guilty of materialism; he holds
"reason" as sacrosanct as Daniyal holds "art," and both are inadequate
as ultimate explanations of the cosmos. They are only valid in so far as
they partake of a spiritual sense:

The spiritual sense, the faculty of spiritual discrimination, must function on a
plane superior to that of the other senses or intuitions because it is the valuator
of those other modes of valuing. It is the co-ordinator of judgments by
standards that otherwise have nothing in common.

Art only becomes great "in the measure that it makes itself the vehicle
of spiritual truth," and the aesthetic sense is subordinated. And at the
back of it all is the idea that "no particular occasion can be judged without reference to the universe as a whole."

With none of this is Smith in agreement; he lacks the cosmic sense.
As a European he believes that an "enlightened sociality is all-in-all";
he fails in detachment because in Europe the different geographical
conditions set up a habit of mind and body "which directs men's
attention outwards and attaches his thoughts to material things." Smith

even rejects Christianity; for his placing of Buddha, Socrates, and Christ on equal terms turns out in the end to be a means of degrading the position of Christ. He is thus against even such a European conception as Sita's, with which he has otherwise much in common. Also he tends to over-emphasise such qualities as aesthetic sensitiveness and sensibility. Amar notes that "a world that honoured [people like Smith] would be a decaying one." And in fact this is true; for one of the virtues of Myers lies in his ability to point to apparently quite dissimilar manifestations of the same spirit. Smith he rightly associates with Daniyal, though he would be prepared to admit a certain difference of degree in value. Nevertheless, fundamentally Smith partakes of the same ethos as Daniyal does; his approach is based on similar conceptions about the nature of man; and in his unwillingness to look beyond material things and his acceptance of worldly standards as ultimate, he provides another type of the same attitude which is responsible for the "deep seated spiritual vulgarity of our age." As Amar says,

There is that which is more important than civilisation; and just as the individual cannot live for himself, so cannot society live for itself, but must keep a self-transcendent ideal before it. Society is not worshipful, nor is humanity. Over and above the immanent there is the transcendent.

Smith worships reason; Daniyal art. Both are ultimately man-made and though Daniyal's 'art' is less worthy of respect than Smith's reason, both ultimately fall down on the same stumbling-block.

This long talk and discussion with Smith may seem to hold up the progress of the book. Nevertheless it has its importance. It brings us round once more to Daniyal: it reinforces certain features of Amar's outlook. And, as usual, Myers is able to clinch his arguments by action. Smith's outlook is not confined to words, and the inadequacy of his philosophical position is shown in his reaction to two religious murders that take place during the journey. To Smith, the fact that Mahomed Fazul, the murderer, should kill a man for "mocking the worship of Allah" is incomprehensible. What, however, moves such a man as Fazul is neither "rational altruism" nor "rational self-interest."

He has no inclination to make himself comfortable in the world; what he prizes and lives by is just that which the apostles of humanism are obliged to ignore or deny.

And though Amar is perhaps hardly correct in assuming that the "case for Mahomed Fazul rests almost wholly upon the character of the man himself," nevertheless his act of murder is one that shows the inadequacy of a purely rational, altruistic approach to human problems. His comment on Smith is very much to the point:

People like Fazul, by the mere fact of their existence, give Smith evidence of the inadequacy of his conception of human nature, and arouse in him an unacknowledged hostility. Smith's intolerance of intolerance is nothing short of fanatical. He does not like to be disturbed in his comfortable belief that the whole human race, if it only knew its own mind a little better, would realize that it wants just what he wants and dislikes just what he dislikes.

The "impartial administrator of the law," for whom Smith stands, is important in civilisation; nevertheless administration has, in addition to its obvious virtues, some less obvious defects: if it prevents chaos, it imposes a subtle type of uniformity that tends to escape notice but that nevertheless deserves consideration.

Finally, between the two, Amar and Smith, there is a great deal of difference in self-knowledge. Despite his flaunting of impartiality, Smith produces an unpleasant sense of unfair-mindedness. He does not realize the importance of his lack of a spiritual sense, whereas Amar is at least sufficiently self-aware to realise that his own aesthetic sense is extremely limited. We agree with his comment:

I cannot believe that my inability to take much interest in works of art *as such* is as dwarfing as Smith's disability.

Once at Kathiapur, Amar is rapidly involved in the minor intrigues of the place. Srilata, his sister, is good-natured; but she tends to accept current valuations in a world where "shallowness is an indispensable requisite in polite conversation." Ambissa is grosser, though as Amar realises, hardly wicked; and he sees in his self-critical way that by refusing to help her ambitions, he would be regarded as "a person more regardful of his own fastidiousness than of the welfare of his kith and kin." A touch of egotism—or the realisation that such an attitude of excessive fastidiousness can, unless one is very careful, slide into egotism—is ever present with Amar.

At Kathiapur various appeals for his help are indeed made, and time and time again the question comes round to Daniyal. In these scenes there is perhaps a tendency for the novel to drag; one seems to be continually promised a climax, and to be as continually put off. That, of course, always tends to be one of Myers's faults. The lack of variation of *pace*, the fact that his stories tend to move at a uniform speed—in a way a mark of his sense of detachment—restricts (in the technical sense) the interest of his novels. The intrigues, because for the most part they are seen through Amar's eyes and because he stands aloof from them, have a curious ineffectual quality. Nevertheless these scenes at Kathiapur are not without their interest. They reveal the character of Amar and reinforce that impression of watchfulness and rejection of the superficial and meretricious. The purposes of Daniyal are continually probed and his character, in his absence, is built up as surely in Lalita's hatred of him, and in Srilata's tempered praise, as in Amar's rejection. Amar, as he himself asserts, "values character above wits," and in fact regards Srilata's attitude to Daniyal as a sort of inverted "priggery"; she denies her natural moral taste because she fears to appear different from her surroundings. At the same time, we see that Amar, as Lalita points out, does not as yet fully understand what he is up against in Daniyal, nor has he realised that "five minutes in your [Amar's] company would be enough to make him [Daniyal] hate you like poison."

During this time, too, Amar is visited constantly by further doubts of his fitness to retire. Contact with Smith had already shown him how his intention must have seemed "selfish and this moment ill chosen" to all except those who agreed with his particular stand-point. A ride with Lalita opens his mind to joys to be lost: "no more riding over the desert, no more delight in physical energy, never again feel the hot, dry air rushing past one's face." A little later the isolation into which he had been withdrawing has turned into loneliness; and the comment is "I still hold firm to my decisions—but not easily, not without doubts." A chance meeting with a Yogi reveals an aspect of 'reality' which Amar has tended to ignore; for as the Yogi says, "those who do not live in contact with reality can do nothing—nothing to promote either evil or good." The point of the meeting is to re-affirm the closeness of the relationship between flesh and spirit; those who are concerned with the spirit cannot ignore completely the things of this world. For distasteful as in many ways the Yogi is, he does in a sense live in contact with reality—or at least near to a reality that Amar is striving to forget.

A little later Amar is stricken with a fever. His illness is to be regarded symbolically; the pills the Yogi gives him help to cure him in more ways than one. They awake his senses so that his hearing, for instance, becomes more acute; they arouse him so that he apprehends more closely the immediate things around him. When Lalita comes to see him during his recovery a significant phrase occurs: "taking flesh and spirit together as one, he found her somehow beautiful"—a phrase that recalls a comment of the Yogi's. Memories of his marriage with Sita return. He sees how early he had begun to detach himself from her: and he considers how "this process had been inevitable, for he had been straining towards something that lay beyond human relationships." The next question he asks himself is significant of a further change in his outlook: "Had this marriage been for her good?—or for his?" He realises that subterranean forces of which he has little knowledge still bind him to Sita:

Ignorance was one of the heaviest fetters of the spirit; and what ignorance could be more dangerous than that of one's own hidden Mind?

From now on self-questionings become more frequent. He realises that in his dealings with Hari and Lalita (his desire to bring them both to a sense of reality) there has been an element of anger, of ill-will that is destroying his solitude and his communings; he is filled with "confusion and speculation where no confusion or speculation should be."

The Rajah's doubts are finally brought into the open at the meeting with Gokal—a reunion which brings us back once more to Gokal's vision. Gokal relates the story of his vision to Amar; he tells that

the thinness of the crust of tangible things, the emptiness of matter, the super-ficiality of appearances, suddenly were revealed.

The smell of water-lilies and the elephant trumpetings, which form part of the dream, connect the scene with Gunevati and Daniyal. The threads which had seemed so loose are now being pulled together. Gokal's vision is a revelation of certain aspects of the evil in Daniyal. The treatment of Gunevati that Amar has witnessed and the threat of the mad elephant which is held over her reveal beneath superficial appearances certain forces which Amar has ignored. Gokal's determination increases, and his speech is now directed towards dissuading Amar from his contemplated retirement. In reply to the question, "You are sure that you are inwardly prepared?" Amar has to admit,

"I am not so sure as I was." The Rajah's voice was bitter. "But prepared or not, I am determined to delay no longer."

Then Gokal reveals that despite the Emperor's concessions and a certain agreement about policy, he can no longer associate himself with Mobarek; the crux of the matter lies in Mobarek's attitude to Daniyal.

His conscience allows him to ally himself with Daniyal in order to obtain from society the ultimate structure he desires. I could not do that. I believe it to be wrong to associate myself with Daniyal even as a measure of expedience.

The issue is now fairly stated. And Gokal further points to the funda-mental flaw in Amar which, he considers, will nullify his desire to with-draw. He considers that Amar has two natures, and that basically he is "A man with a deep intuition of godhead, and a craving to address himself to a personal god." His Buddhism springs from "the reaction of another part of [his] nature against this basic tendency" in order to satisfy "the peculiar demands of [his] theorizing self."

The energies and impulses that gave it birth are personal, jealous, and feminine,—so that in point of fact this cold impersonal philosophy of yours is the child and darling of an all-too-human heart.

Amar, in fact, has repressed the more important part of his nature—

"the heart"—and he is accused of being more like Smith than he himself thinks. Gokal emphasises that the world is "an arena for the very highest spiritual and moral struggle." He urges Amar to be guided by his intuition rather than by his philosophy. "I want you to obey your instincts in regard to Daniyal." For spiritual values do *not* exist "apart from personalities." And then, in the discussion that follows, Gokal reveals Daniyal as *wicked*. Amar argues that he is trivial. And Gokal points out that

if triviality takes an important place in the world, if it is the chief barrier between men and God, then triviality is important.

The conscious sinner at least acknowledges God: but

the man who is incapable of an emotional response to the universe in its august or divine aspect—that man is indeed beyond the pale.

Then comes his analysis of wickedness and evil:

Trivial-mindedness in individuals or communities is practically the whole of what I mean by evil, for in the end it leads to the ultimate offence against God. What the wicked man looks for in human suffering is the spectacle of God being mocked, rightness being set at naught, the world being made to seem a place of purposeless evil, a triumph of the diabolic over the good.

Evil lies in the offence done to the creator, "the humiliation done to Goodness Itself." Gokal stresses the fundamental sympathy of outlook which binds Smith and Daniyal together. For, "it is not the machinery of civilisation, but the informing spirit of the social unit that keeps it alive and in health" despite Smith's reforming zeal. What matters is what lies beneath the surface, the transcendental ideal. Justice and altruism too often spring from jealousy, envy, and self-interest: "lovers of mankind in and for itself are primarily haters of God." When Amar urges practicability, Gokal points out that no man can decide what is practicable. Above all: "Man is under an obligation to act—under the psychological necessity that is also a spiritual obligation."

And so Amar visits Daniyal, and the book moves towards its climax. The argument is clinched in action. The incident of Dantawat, a member of the Camp who, driven by Daniyal's neglect, attempts to commit suicide, prepares us for worse. The Rajah realises Daniyal's cultivation of flippancy, and appreciates that he moves in a world of arbitrary inclinations "without affection or pity." At the meeting Daniyal taunts Amar about his wife; and then, in all its 'triviality' comes the incident of the cat. Daniyal, in Amar's presence, has been juggling with some balls. A white cat rubs against his leg, causing him to miss his catch. Frowning, the prince places his foot on the cat's head:

Then with a swift and smiling glance at his spectators he slowly pressed his foot down. One after another the bones in the cat's head could be heard to crack. . . . The cat's paws were beating the air; its body rose stiffly in an arc and then collapsed in spasms; a little pool of blood spread out upon the floor.

A certain smallness and pettiness in the action conveys the extent of Daniyal's evil. In a flash Amar's decision is made. He acts. As he strikes at Daniyal the whole effort of the book is resolved.

When Gokal takes Amar back across the lake after Daniyal's guards have struck the Rajah down, the Brahmin reflects on a "destiny that had perhaps been inescapable." Myers has answered Amar's problem. Action *is* a spiritual necessity in the face of the evil of the world.

The tone of *Rajah Amar* is significantly different from that of *Prince Jali*. The earlier book is full of question, the searching of a boy in the face of experience. The former specialises in a poised assurance, reflecting the irony of the Rajah's speculations, an assurance that breaks down because of the growth of an inner uncertainty leading to fuller experience. Just as the claims of the world become apparent to Jali when he sees Gunevati terribly mutilated, so the need to act in the face of vileness is made clear to Amar by Daniyal's behaviour with the cat. In both books the search for a stabilised order, a coherent attitude that will take in both God and Mammon resolves itself in a decision that even the self-consciously superior must play their parts in the affairs of men. Distinction of mind and soul is insufficient to make the individual self-contained. The teaching of the Guru in *The Pool of Vishnu* that

the knowledge gained in communion and ripened in solitude must pour its life into the world through action

is foreshadowed. The theme of the novel, conveyed in a nice integration of speculation and action, becomes unequivocal at these key points. This indeed is the flower that must spring from such roots.

Obviously then, there is an immense advance from *The Orissers*. The baffling problem of the Orissers in their remoteness from the world is reaching a solution which necessitates certain concessions to that world. The emotional response to the immediate situation demands satisfaction. What intuition, refined by an analysis based on a sense of severe intellectual and moral standards, a consciousness of superior worth, apprehends in contact with the worldlings which the ordinary processes of society throw into prominence, places the 'fastidious' under obligations that exclude the selfish desire to retire. At the same time, the worldly powers must not be underrated. What may be spiritually worthless can yet be politically and socially of great authority. The 'trivial' are immensely powerful. In this trilogy, which is mainly, and admittedly, further exploratory of the position of an Orisser-group, the more spiritually aware of the characters are not conspicuously successful in their political and social interventions. The more positive modes of social behaviour, indeed, belong to the sequel, *The Pool of Vishnu*. For the moment Myers is content to affirm the necessity of intervention. Despite his later acceptance of the notion of the natural goodness of man, Myers's ethical ideas so far involve the necessary conflict of good and evil rather than the possibility of the *refinement* of the evil by the good in accordance with certain notions of personal relationships; thus Amar strikes at Daniyal. In an altered context conflict yields to persuasion in accordance with a new vision of the possibilities inherent in all human personalities. But the working out of that theme belongs to the next book. At the moment, however, the 'near' and the 'far'—the immediate and the transcendental—are required to be mutually interactive, so that society shall be spiritualised, and a morality, based on transcendental standards, shall appreciate its responsibilities towards the world of men. *The Root and the Flower* reveals the basic apartness of human beings, to which retreat out of life is no answer. The effort at integration comes in the sequel.

The Root and the Flower, then, as I began by saying, is Myers's masterpiece. That there are certain weaknesses of construction must be admitted; the book indeed involves a number of probings of a theme rather than a defined and assured centrality. It is, that is to say, deficient in form; and there is development without resolution. It is still deficient, too, in 'felt life', though to a much lesser extent than *The Orissers* was. Nevertheless it presents an astonishingly wide purview of modern civilisation. It shows a remarkable capacity to detect basic similarities of outlook between apparently disparate manifestations of mental attitude. It explores its themes with a pertinacity and a clear mental sightedness rarely approached in modern literature. As Professor D. W. Harding says, in the essay published in *Scrutiny* mentioned above, Myers's best novels "instead of being an *expression* of problems and beliefs, are rather a means in themselves of defining the problems and clarifying the beliefs." This is certainly so in *The Root and the Flower*. The whole of 'civilised' life is brought into question from a point of view which assumes that man is a rational creature and which presupposes a certain standard of emotional and intellectual integrity against which the 'good' and the 'bad' characters can be measured. A certain coldness of tone in itself explicitly reinforces standards of intelligence inhibiting to emotional over-exuberance and helps to foster those aspects of civilised life the incidents reveal; the consciously organised 'literary' writing is the counterpart of a conscious exploration of themes in which the author is deeply, but not obtrusively, involved. The incidents are sufficiently 'thrilling' and 'exciting' to make the novel 'readable' in the Sunday reviewer's sense of the term and at the same time to create a fine sense of relevance between the coarse political life of the times and the problems of the protagonists.

The main themes are those of the "true self"—and the intense spiritual struggle involved in probing the depths of one's true nature so that one can arrive at some form of inner equilibrium based on self-knowledge—and the necessities and difficulties of "contact" with other people. Yet cutting oneself off may blind one to certain parts of one's own personality—the full development of personality, in Myers's view, can only be achieved in relation to one's fellows. Thus certain types of religious consciousness, for instance, are rejected by implication because they abstract the individual from his social responsibilities. (It is interesting to speculate that Myers himself, for all his criticisms of the conception, falls for the same idea as Smith, the humanist, that an "enlightened sociality" is all in all—though the particular connotation involved in the word 'enlightened' is what marks the difference between the two and what justifies Myers's criticism of the humanist position. Certainly Myers interestingly and unconsciously illustrates the difficulties of developing the religious consciousness in our age; in his handling of them, 'transcendental' conceptions take on a somewhat tenuous and ill-defined appearance. All that is really involved is his belief that there is something—that something being subject to no theological definition—beyond man.) In the last resort, as we shall see, Myers was more successful in probing and defining the problem at the individual than at the social level. His belief, pervasive throughout the book, that social policies exist only in terms of personalities carries with it certain simplifications, a subjectivism which militates against a complete and assured handling of the complex themes inherent in the dichotomy of man and society.

For the rest, subtle affinities between apparently very different types of refinement and animality are revealed with magnificent insight and an exactingness that implies a firm grasp by the author within his spheres of assumption. It is, in fact, ultimately the mind of the author which supplies such 'form' as the novel possesses, something *inherent* in the total atmosphere of the work rather than something objectively patterned in the relation of incidents and characters. In this there is perhaps something lost in 'impersonality'; but, when that has been said, *The Root and the Flower* remains a work which, it seems to me, has only been excelled among English writing during the present century by the best works of James, Conrad, and Lawrence.

The writing still remains 'literary'; Myers never achieved that capacity to 'feel into' language which marks the greatest novelists. What I mean can perhaps best be illustrated by quotation and analysis:

The hot noontide hush would be lying upon the land—upon the plains, the deserts, the forests, upon the whole of India and beyond, if only one's fancy could picture it. In that hush he moved and loitered and halted; he listened to it and felt it engulfing him in a vastness that was without bounds. He looked up into the thirsty foliage, he listened, he peered, he followed with his eyes the irresolute fall of a leaf. Flimsy and tattered was all the shade that these poor branches could now give; and alas for the green and sappy things that had trusted to their protection! Alas for the mosses and grasses and cool-veined plants, alas for the delicate bushes, huddling vainly in patches of ground that had once been moist, in crevices that had once looked safe! The furious sun, by sheer persistence, had broken through to them, turning them suddenly into skeletons; and it was these beautiful silvery skeletons that now invested the wood with its air of magical desiccation, and by the clinking of their fairy bones filled it with its peculiar silky rustle. That rustle!—hark to it now!—rushing past, like a flight of ghosts, upon the hot wind's breath.

The passage is taken from *Prince Jali*. The mood of dreary scepticism, so typical of Myers, has descended on Jali; it marks his realisation of failure to integrate himself. But there is lacking that close correspondence between the description and the state of mind which would serve to define, uniquely, the emotional situation. The short, sharp phrases "he listened, he peered, he followed . . ." etc., are not immediately relevant to the heat and the "dreary sceptical" spirit of Jali. The repeated "alas for" has the air of a literary device, a *conscious* evocation of weariness, instead of a uniquely conveyed and imposed feeling; and the 'literary' sense of the passage is increased by the use of such consciously romantic adjectives as 'silvery', 'magical', 'fairy', 'silky'. The repeated exclamation marks give an insistence, as if the passage has not sufficiently done its work, and the author felt the need for an emphasis the words themselves had not provided. It has, in fact, nothing fresh to offer in its exploration of this mood; it seems to result from taking thought about the elements which would to the author's mind best coalesce with the required mood; there is nothing of inevitability about it. Yet throughout the book the style always remains competent, if external. The story flows, if too evenly. And, cumulatively an atmosphere is built up.

One other point of interest remains. Myers had never been to India, and his account of Eastern modes of thought depends entirely on his reading. Indian students have informed me that they consider his account very creditable for a westerner; but it is obvious that his appreciation, if what has just been said about the comparative vagueness of his religious ideas is accepted, must inevitably fall short of a full and intimate apprehension. Concern for eastern ideas is, of course, one of the marks of the eclecticism of our age; with the decay of Christian dogmatic beliefs we have sought consolation in what at best must be an inadequate comprehension—because we are not 'of' the culture—of other religious approaches. This eclecticism points, perhaps, to one more aspect of our decaying moral order; it makes the particularly 'subjective' emphasis of Myers just mentioned more than usually difficult to transcend because there is no assured moral or religious tradition within which the writer can work. His own personal integrity inevitably bears too heavy a burden because there is no body of vital ideas and beliefs in the society of our time on which he can depend.

CHAPTER IV

"THE POOL OF VISHNU"

ALTHOUGH *The Pool of Vishnu*[1] was not published until 1940 and thus appeared after *Strange Glory*, which came four years earlier, it will be more convenient to consider the later novel first, as it forms a sequel to *The Root and the Flower*.

The education of the young Jali continues in *The Pool of Vishnu*, though he does not play a very active part in the novel. The main relationships involved are those of Hari and Sita and of Mohan and Damayanti. After Amar's disastrous encounter with Daniyal, and consequent blinding, news comes that Salim's cavalry threatens to sever communications, and in an attempt to reach Vidyapur, of which Amar is Rajah, the little party flee. On their journey they take refuge in a half-ruined castle, and rest there a while. In a reckless mood, induced by his growing dissatisfaction with his relationship with Sita, Hari joins in a struggle against Salim's men, and is wounded. A little later Hari sets out to accompany Jali on a visit to Bhoj, Rajah of Daulatpur, and his wife, Lakshmi. On the way they fall in with the holy man, the Guru, who forms so important an element in the book. Hari has temporarily succumbed to his wound, but the care of the Guru restores him. Jali continues to Daulatpur, where he receives a further introduction to the 'world'. He becomes friendly, however, with Mohan, Bhoj's elder brother, who has given up the throne to Bhoj, and (partly at the instigation, and with the help, of the Guru) is devoting his time to practising, within his limited means, a new mode of social organisation. Mohan is in love with Damayanti, daughter of a neighbouring Rajah, who, a widower, selfishly clings to her. The working out of this relationship, again with the help of the Guru's ideas, forms the focal point of the book. There are many vicissitudes; but the pair form a stable relationship, for Vishnu is the preserver, and it is the pool of Vishnu that symbolically represents the theme of this final volume. Hari is assassinated, Amar, blinded by Daniyal's guard, has joined a band of pilgrims, Gokal and Sita disappear from sight. At the end, the young man Jali returns to the palace at Agra, where the novel began.

---

[1] Myers had some difficulty over the title. Originally he intended to call the book 'The Treasure and the Serpent'. The point is worth noting because of the significance which antithetical titles possessed for Myers, pointing to his sense of the dichotomy between the body and the spirit, the material and the transcendental, that which exists in time and the timeless.

The Pool of Vishnu involves an arabesque of personal relationships. It sets out the positive conceptions of Myers, at the centre of which stands his idea of the "personal." Most of the story is told objectively; but part of it is related in the form of Jali's diary; and part of it involves a fuller revelation of a story told to the Guru.

Hari feels that his relationship with Sita has become void of content. After a meeting together, Gokal analyses Hari's motives in desiring death. He seeks a way out of the impasse of the triangle—Sita, Amar, and himself: "Men delight in destruction as much as in creation, in pain as much as in pleasure." Hari's irresponsibility is stressed, first in his seeking relief by joining the soldiers to fight Salim's men: "Self-consciousness was alive in him only in the thought; 'I am not thinking. What a relief!' " and then in fighting on the wrong side: " 'Well!' he thought, 'Life is like that. And the responsibility is not mine.' " Sita is feeling the strain. She stands between Amar and Hari. She realises that Hari needs something to guide him through life, but diagnoses him as simpler than in fact, as Gokal points out, he is. But the Hari-Amar-Sita triangle serves chiefly to set the stage by drawing attention to a problem. Gokal realises the nature of the situation:

"Here we are—Sita, and Jali, and I—here we are—together, alive, and with love in our hearts! But something swathes, and clouds, and muffles us. Even I, who see what is happening, can do nothing. . . . There is love, but love is not understanding. Why do neither Jali nor Hari speak to her as they do to me."

What, then, is involved in the love relationship? How can those who love each other yet find their love threatened by lack of understanding? What deeper resources of the human psyche need to be drawn on to make relationship a success? For human beings—and human relationships—matter. Gokal recalls that for Sita, "the touchstone of reality was apprehensibleness":

This was, of course, to place the human being at the centre of things. But wasn't it only common sense to do that? For what meaning could one find in the word reality unless it meant reality for human beings?

Hari's problem, then, is the first to be used as a means of exploring the nature of relationship. At the Guru's cell, where uncle and nephew stay together, Hari still fails to find the desired solution to his affair with Sita, although Amar has now retired from the world. He admits that his life is disordered and discusses his problem with the Guru. The Guru suggests a solution to him and the first of the many discussions on the subject of personal relationships takes place. The Guru asks him if he has discussed the matter with Sita. Hari says that he has not "because it would offend [his] taste." And then the Guru sets out the germ of the idea that is to be the basic conception of the book:

"It seems to me that half the trouble that arises between human beings is caused by lack of consideration. A man imagines that he is the other's superior. . . . He assumes responsibilities that he ought to share, he makes concealments, he will not ask of the other what he asks of himself or apply to the other the same standards. The man who says to himself that the other wouldn't understand, or couldn't bear to face the truth, or would be made too angry by it, is really being protective not of the other but of himself."

What stands in his way is lack of "moral courage."

But Hari cannot take the advice in its relationship to Sita. He is in the grip of "Fear-in-itself"—the "hell into which you sink *alone.*" He lacks "spirit." So he returns to the court of Akbar. There, by a method of buffoonery somewhat similar to that of Harry in *The 'Clio'*, he 'succeeds'; he reconciles Akbar to Salim and becomes (incidentally by using in his own robust way some of the Guru's advice by being honest and open with Akbar) a favourite of the Emperor, though one feels that in doing so he descends to the Emperor's level. For he can never be completely sincere—and in this book, despite his pleasant side, he comes to be associated more with the worldlings than with Amar, Jali, Gokal, and Sita. As the Guru says:

His first impulse is always to produce an effect. He can't bear not to make something of an occasion just as an occasion;

and Jali considers that it is as if there were "something in the air of Agra that turns people into play-actors—and Hari won't give up posturing even when in danger of his life." Continuity with the earlier book is suggested in Jali's reminiscence to the Guru of the advice Hari had given him at the opening of *The Root and the Flower*; and the comment the Guru makes clearly implies the new values that are to take the place of posturings and false appearances. He reveals the fundamental split in Hari's character:

By nature he is sensitive and diffident, and easily impressed by appearances; so in order to cope with the world he began early in life to dress himself up. He has acted his assumed character with a good deal of success; but at a cost that no-one can afford.

In the scene at Agra we see this posturing of Hari in action; Jali's comment is symptomatic of the growing maturity of the young prince:

The world of public affairs resembled nothing more than a monstrous schoolroom in which grown-up children were playing with brightly-coloured and very dangerous toys.

Here Hari's "spectacular, semi-barbaric style of living" suits his "newly-developed political role—and . . . his gifts, which included a pretty sense of buffoonery." And so Hari never becomes a fully developed person; his life in the "unreal world" of political chicanerie has "already blunted his sense of reality," or at least caused him to ignore it by a deliberate act of will. So death is his lot—brought on by his own indiscretions in the "world." He is assassinated.

Certain features of Myers's theories have already emerged in his treatment of the character: there is the demand for personal, inner sincerity, the reassertion of the "unreality" of the world. Hari's failure is to be set against the greater success of the other relationship of the book. As the Guru says: "Many people are satisfied to communicate with one another merely as members of a type, but the personal spirit in you cares for something else." Herein lies Hari's fault. His fear springs from within himself; he should put his love for Sita to the test of candour, the test of the relation of person to person. He does not do so. It is with this test that we shall be concerned from now on; faith is an activity involving the courage of spiritually aware persons. Amar's retirement, too, foreshadows a life in community which indicates the further possibilities of true relationship. His dismissal is perhaps a trifle perfunctory —a device of plot as much as an integral part of the theme. Nevertheless, significantly, his retirement is one in community, not one in isolation. When he joins the pilgrims self-consciousness relaxes; and though at times the people around him become inanimate surroundings only, circumstances not persons, yet when he returns from these spiritual absences, he finds a new communion with his fellows. This is the sign of his inner emancipation—"the power to mix with his fellow-men without pride, without pretence, without concealment, and without shame."

The rest of the book is largely made up of Jali's relationship with Lakshmi and Bhoj and with Mohan and Damayanti. Through them his education is continued and completed. Rajah Bhoj represents a much more refined version of Daniyal; he completely lacks the vulgar ostentation of the prince, yet ultimately the two are spiritually akin. For in Bhoj the very careful lack of ostentation is in itself paradoxically only a form of display. Jali visits Bhoj and his wife. The palace in which they live is symbolic of the type of life they lead:

It was at once surrounded by, and extremely remote from, the common habitations of men. He knew no other palace that was not set apart, removed from the swarming populace, but this dark, ancient building was shouldered by the poor, whose squalid hovels clung, like swallows' nests, to its thick, frowning walls. Not a sound could come through those isolating depths of stone; and if you cared to remember that an outside world existed, that consciousness only enhanced your sense of privileged seclusion.

The sense of privacy, of being cut off by an exaggerated sense of tradition and formality that the palace suggests (the symbolism is almost too insistent) is transferred to its owner, Bhoj. "Formality, indeed, was the Rajah's chief characteristic." His life is stereotyped in terms of the past: "'History repeats itself' he would say, meaning that it should." The Rajah and his wife are examples of a particular kind of highly self-conscious, cultivated people whose outlook is nevertheless concerned only with the past. Their culture is evident; and their sense of their own importance, although worn lightly, is nevertheless there. "Lightly as these people wore their importance, that importance everywhere proclaimed itself."

At first, Jali feels himself increase in stature as a result of the patronage of his new friends. Bhoj treats him as an equal; he conveys a sense of tradition, of cultivated existence which makes Daulatpur compare favourably with the environment of the Emperor. Lakshmi possesses great self-control and charm of manner, dignity and serenity. Yet, as Jali soon discovers, there is something wrong.

What is lacking is what should come from the inner life. Bhoj and Lakshmi stand for the cultivation of the outward form, the social gesture, at the expense of the inner light, the spontaneous being. Their desire is always to live up to a certain social standard, to see themselves in a certain setting; what is involved is a more refined form of Hari's posturing. For in spite of all Lakshmi's outward composure, she lacks inner serenity. Once more, though more subtly than heretofore, we are examining an accepted convention of existence, instead of a genuine living from the 'real' self. Even at the very first, Jali is aware that Lakshmi lives "in a constant state of tension, although she never gave a direct sign of it . . . perhaps, indeed, it was the very stillness of her body, the tranquillity of her gaze, the perfect timing of both her movements and her speech, that gave him his clue." Like Henry James's Madame Merle, she is "too perfectly the social animal."

The implications of this emerge when Jali begins to get over his admiration. One of the feelings that the palace gives, as we have seen, is that of a "privileged seclusion," a sense of being lifted above the fret and care of ordinary life. But this sheltered way of life has its dangers for personal integrity. Jali cannot help noticing the rewards of a ruling class; not only in money, but in the "profound self-esteem, the deep sense of one's inward worth, that accompanied the Rajah's way of thinking."

They lived fair-seeming lives; there was nothing slack, nothing gross, nothing tasteless in Bhoj or Lakshmi; they had courage, self-control, energy, and pride; but there was something fundamentally wrong.

A form of subtle egotistical self-flattery marks the Rajah's attitude. In a later talk with Damayanti Jali sets out Bhoj's view:

Bhoj thinks that for all time there should be a few very wise and rich and cultured men (like himself) at the top of society, and progressively less wisdom and less wealth, and less culture as you go down the social scale.

Contact with the Guru and comment from him increase Jali's sense of uneasiness. When he expresses his desire to be like Bhoj, the Guru tells him to be like himself: "Don't complicate things for yourself by trying to be, or pretending to be, what you are not." Jali compares Bhoj and Lakshmi with his father's court, and notes the lack of "freedom for spontaneous movements of the mind and heart." In fact here,

everyone laboured under an unceasing self-consciousness, self-constraint, and strain. These people were the slaves of their own social standards. . . . A woman like Lakshmi was concerned to keep up appearances every instant of the day—and not only for the benefit of others, but to satisfy her own private self-esteem.

What is involved, then, is the erection of a social picture of oneself which creates an inner sense of strain and self-consciousness. The desire to live up to a preconceived 'persona', the element of self-dramatisation in social life as opposed to the *natural* response of personality to person-ality, is something to be condemned. The creation of a sham personality causes that feeling of strain which is one of the chief characteristics of our civilisation. One remembers Lawrence's condemnation of the social beings in Galsworthy. In Richard Hillary's *The Last Enemy* one is told of the creation of a social myth, and the consequent perversion of effort involved in living up to it. The endeavour to discover the essential beneath all the accretions of social habit is not, of course, as we have noted, an uncommon one among intellectuals. At a time when social criteria of behaviour and action are more powerful than ever before, the integrity of the few has been directed to discovery of essential self. What makes Myers's contribution significant is the delicacy and sub-tlety of the analysis of highly 'civilised' and yet unsatisfactory types; thus one appreciates that Myers's analysis of the cult of 'first-rateness' has its value in one's attempt, for instance, to define the unsatisfactori-ness of the Parisian 'civilisation' which Henry James presents in *The Ambassadors*. And there is great interest attaching to the way of life, ex-pressed in mimic in the novel, Myers proposes in its stead. Lakshmi, presenting a picture "not of what she was but of what she longed to be," lived in an atmosphere of continual *strain*.

It was certainly very hard to imagine what Lakshmi's naked personality—her central self stripped of all pretence—would be like.

What Myers wants is a new and fresh response to each social situation, a bringing into play of the genuine personality, as the artist who achieves anything really good responds afresh to what he writes about or paints. In fact it might almost be said that Myers put forward the conception of the 'social artist', as opposed to the social copyist: the standard was to be created anew by bringing into play all the resources of personality: the danger was a mere copying of the Old Masters, a sort of academy style of life.

Jali, then, grows to dislike these people. He finds that he doesn't like "the person he became when in their company." Basically, there is only everlasting sameness; even their nonchalance is conscious art. And at the back is a devastating boredom. There is something lacking—"not courage, not exactly character—something more common and necessary," as Jali says to Damayanti. The underlying corruption of Bhoj's outlook is seen in his attitude to the Sesodia, an important Indian potentate. Lakshmi and he wish to visit the Sesodia, not because he is an interesting person, or a delightful companion, but because he occupies a commanding social position. They accept, that is to say, not the *person* but the position. Their culture is largely a matter of pretence, so that they can persuade themselves that they really deserve the privileges they allocate to themselves. As Damayanti says: "All those graces become worthless—become tainted—in the absence of a certain saving grace which they lack." What the Rajah and his wife lack is magnanimity and generous feeling. Jali considers that despite their discipline, dignity, and public-spiritedness, "the intelligence of the heart has been suffocated." Their outlook is similar to that of the English in E. M. Forster's *A Passage to India*. Bhoj perhaps has the feeling that "the position [he occupies] ought not to exist at all." "His life is spent in an effort to compensate with virtues, graces, and charities for something to which he knows he has no right," says Damayanti. Why then do they attach so much value to "appearances," to the "look of the thing"? Lakshmi has surrounded herself with the very best things; the second-rate is "her secret bugbear." She worships at the altar of the "First-rate."

The devotees of the First-rate just pay tribute here, there, and everywhere . . . All . . . she assesses in the same currency.

And that, as Damayanti remarks, is not first-rate. All the time they are afraid of appearing second-rate. "They are afraid of each other. They have not the courage of their convictions, and so accept the world's opinion. They do not answer to the voice of [their] spontaneous being." So Randhir, a young man who makes a passing appearance in the novel and who is killed in battle, has given his life "for the sake of making a fine gesture," a gesture in the political struggle over the throne in which he has no personal interest, but to which he has been driven by a wife and a mother who believe in such a panache. As the Guru points out, there are things in the world worth dying for—but Randhir has not chosen the right thing:

> No doubt Randhir was telling himself that he was going to his death for the sake of his own pride and self-respect. Ought I to have said to him: "Randhir, what is the value of this pride and self-respect, when, having no roots in anything outside themselves, they bring no vital sap"?

The effect is to turn a man into a play-actor.

Among the most potent influences in current social life are feminine values, which reign so much in the palace. His wife and mother have sent Randhir to his doom. When the Guru comes to play his part in the story of Damayanti and Mohan, he appreciates that Damayanti is sacrificing more than Mohan is, when she abandons the palace:

> In a woman's life essential human values, social values, and sexual values are tangled up in a very complicated way. Compared with a man, a woman has much more to lose and, ostensibly, much less to gain, by being unworldly.

The world expects the woman to trade on the fact that she is a woman, and therefore she is much more involved in social values than a man; for in acting up to the world's expectation, she must necessarily take over the values the world gives her; thus she relies on them for her self-confidence to an even greater extent than do men. The social and the sexual are inextricably bound together. Hence arise Damayanti's difficulties and hence her need, not for self-sacrifice, but for self-conquest. She has to fight against both the tension of family and sexual ties and of social competitiveness, so that she may "follow her own light"; and her remarkableness in personality springs from her victory over the insidious social and sexual ties.[1]

Bhoj and Lakshmi, then, provide something of the background just as, at a much lower level of depravity, Daniyal and his Pleasance did in the previous book: "This is the great world which sweeps along intoxicated by its own posturings." But this world is not easy to avoid, and its values being pervasive, a great effort of the personality, a fundamental reordering of the individual are essential if its values are to be seen in their true light. As we have seen, Jali, realising his immaturity, is at first taken in by Bhoj and Lakshmi:

[1] A French critic, M. Denis Saurat, has drawn attention to Myers's realisation of the power exercised by women on social behaviour: "En particulier, Myers révèle à vif, et plus qu'aucun romancier, le rôle dominateur de la femme dans notre société." (*Spectateur*, 14 Jan., 1947.) It is such acuteness of analysis that provides a measure of Myers's insight into social relationships and of his sureness of moral outlook. His books, if no more, are among the most remarkable social documents of the time, and show how much less adequate are such people as the Webbs and Bernard Shaw as social critics. Compare, too, the subtlety of his analysis of certain aristocratic types with the superficiality of Dickens's Sir Leicester and Lady Dedlock in *Bleak House*, who exist so largely in terms of a formula.

The ironical lights in Lakshmi's eyes, the placid tones of Bhoj's voice, seemed to him now to be tokens of an unshakable strength.

There are times, too, when Jali yields to the forces of social pressure around him. Even when he has reacted against them, rather priggishly perhaps, he still feels the desire to stand well in the opinion of the great world. When he visits Agra, despite his awareness of the self-importance of the court officials riding their metaphorical 'elephants', he sets about to produce the right impression. He confesses:

Thus at every point I sacrificed those whom I love and respect in order to gain a little esteem from those whom I do not.

And so, as he comments:

what Peter did under fear of death we do hourly under the fear of a shrug or a raised eyebrow, and are hardly aware of doing it.

Nor is Jali the only one who has to struggle against the imposition by the world of a set social pattern or who fails to lead a 'spontaneous' existence. The Guru himself, in his early days, had been tempted by his fame and by his reputation as a holy man to give way to pride. On one occasion he failed to satisfy a man who came to him for help; and when he searched for the cause he realised that he needed help and comfort himself:

He [the man] wanted reciprocation, and that I would not admit. Beneath all my friendliness there was a small, hard kernel of pride—I was afraid of true comradeship.

The Guru goes on to point out that "the most powerful of appetites is the craving for consideration; and the most powerful of fears is the fear of losing consideration." He himself had been subject to such fears; and even Akbar, despite his position and his strength of character, is a prey to the same temptation. That public life is demoralising is Myers's most constant themes. It always involves an element of make-believe. Mohan, and, as we have seen, Damayanti, too, have been similarly tempted. Thus, Mohan seeks to 'manage' the peasants with whom he wishes to appear equal, instead of entering into a true relationship with them. He finds that to give up habits of mind—reflected often in tricks of manner—that one has acquired through a sense of superiority is difficult; and the Guru criticises Mohan's quiet dignity when the peasants wish to take some of his money away—a dignity which makes them draw away from him as from a superior person. The residues of superiority are very subtle; they may be reflected in a nod. The pervasive tendency in our society to find oneself only in and through other people—to accept exclusively social criteria of behaviour—is shown to involve subtle corruptions of man's nature.

It is one of the signs of Myers's maturity that in no way does he attempt to hide the difficulties of the positive way of life he desires in the place of this social insincerity. It may be thought at first that what is being offered is a facile emotionalism, a sort of warm 'togetherness' of a rather vague and woolly kind. The idea of the natural goodness of man, on which Myers bases his positive ideas, has been corrupted by well-meaning but emotionally unfastidious people; it has provided an excuse for a great deal of loose thinking and inadequate practice. The urge has been towards "complete self-development and complete self-expression," as Mr Clive Bell expresses it in his work on *Crvilisation*— a sense of sin is "nothing more than a remnant of barbarism, which would yield to treatment." But freedom sought in such terms is illusory because no-one can be brought up in an intellectual and emotional vacuum; the influences are either good or bad, and when judging which is which, an aphorism of Myers's to the effect that "there are faults more serious than an honest narrow-mindedness" may well spring to mind.

The last sentence should indeed serve as a warning that Myers most explicitly is not to be found among the ranks of the woolly minded. There is no hint, for instance, of an Oxford Group "sharing" about his conception of personal relationships. There are standards in emotional education as well as in intellectual; his sense of the extraordinary power of society, of the vast incubus that lies upon the human consciousness, would in itself prevent his regarding any solution to our problems in easy terms. Although in the first place he demands a rejection of false social standards, Myers does not favour irresponsibility; what he realises as necessary is a subjection to a new and different discipline, not the overthrowing of restraints in the facile hope that the resultant vacuum will be somehow superior. There is no hint of sentimentality in his conception of 'good' characters—in itself a considerable literary achievement, for it is notoriously more difficult, as most of the nineteenth-century novelists found, to conceive 'goodness' than evil. We know so much about the latter; the former, to be emotionally acceptable by mature minds, can only be satisfactory if the necessary element of rigour and the clear-sighted realisation of difficulties are introduced. What is important, in fact, about the idea that man is by nature inherently good is not the idea in itself, which could well recommend itself to sentimentalists of every kind, but the manner in which the idea is worked out, and the type and standard of human existence it leads the holder to sanction. If, and I must admit that it appears to my mind to be so, the doctrine of original sin is a superior premise to work from, that is not to say that it is not possible to attain acceptable results when working

from an opposed conception. And he who believes in the natural goodness of man perhaps gains on his more pessimistic fellow in the possession of an emotional certitude that is of great assistance in his grim and
weary struggle to attain that perfection of being which he feels in-
tuitively to be attainable; for like Sita and Amar, Myers "recognised
imperfection and aimed at perfection."

The new order is hinted at symbolically in the difference between the
palace of Bhoj and the pleasantness and unconventionality of the home
of Mohan and Damayanti. Little scenes conjure up an entirely different
sort of mental outlook—the charming picture of the child, Santri, playing with her pet, the attitude of the servants, the atmosphere of the
house (the Old Summer Palace). "An agreeable shabbiness met his eye
everywhere." To understand more fully the nature of human relationship which Myers posits in place of the 'socialised' existence, it is necessary to examine in detail the story of Mohan and Damayanti and the
influence of the Guru on their life together. For the right personal
existence and the right personal relationship are intended to have a far-
reaching effect on public life; and they are involved to Mohan's approach to the peasants, and in the Guru's advice to Akbar. An examination of the Father-Damayanti-Mohan embroglio will be a prerequisite,
then, to our understanding of Myers's wider political and social views.

Damayanti, engaged to be married to Akbar, whom she doesn't
know and doesn't love, is deeply attached to her father; and the marriage is really a means by which she can attain an assured social position
and at the same time look after her father for a long period of each year.
Then Mohan, brother of Bhoj and the emissary of the Emperor, meets
Damayanti and the two fall in love. It becomes necessary to sort out the
tangled emotional relationship of the three, Mohan, Damayanti, and
her father. Naturally, the Rajah does not want his daughter to achieve
a genuine love match; that would mean losing her, and his love is a
selfish possessive one:

The Rajah could not contemplate his daughter's making this—or indeed any
other love-match—without rage and despair. Her alliance with the Emperor
commended itself to him most of all for the reason that her feelings would not
be involved.

And he knows how to work on her feelings—by sham illnesses, by
playing on her childish fear of him, for,

fear, the unreasoning anxious fear that one inherits from one's childhood's
days, was able to blend itself most strangely with pity and love.

Nevertheless the pull towards Mohan is strong. In addition to her love
for him, other feelings enter the situation:

Her heart had a conscience that her mind did not understand, and her heart often said to her: "If you give up Mohan you will despise yourself for the rest of your life. . . . Make this renunciation and your reward will be the death of your heart; . . . underneath . . . there will be self-contempt."

The struggle is not easy and Damayanti wavers. She consults the Guru, who makes plain to her the basis of a true relationship. She should only marry Mohan if she really wants to; otherwise she will make him suffer because her self-sacrifice will make her feel superior. The relationship would thus be a false one. Myers is always critical of self-sacrifice; what he prefers is self-conquest. The Guru maintains that Damayanti will treat either her father or Mohan as an inferior if she goes to either without spontaneously wanting to:

> My child, have you never heard the saying: 'The holy man and we are one in kind'. That saying expresses the right view of human nature. It implies: first, that there is but one moral law, and secondly, that that moral law applies to all. This is very important, for it means that it is not true that there is a superior kind of person to whom one standard applies, and another kind of person to whom another standard applies. You would not only be wanting in respect for your father, but acting on a wrong view of humanity altogether, if you were not to apply to him the same high standard that you apply to yourself.

The basis of the true relationship is becoming clearer. It is one of "perfect equality and frankness"; to give in to another's wishes against one's own deeply felt desires is not a glorious self-sacrifice but a relegation of that other to an inferior place; and, the Guru points out, one usually makes such people suffer. What the Guru wants is the plain unadorned self in action, for "in making one's personal life satisfactory, one automatically makes one's public life satisfactory too." I shall have more to say about this later; for the moment it is enough to realise certain implications for the individual. It is to be noticed how strongly Myers bases personal *relationships* on *individual* feeling. Relationship must not mean sacrifice of the individual integrity; of that Myers is strongly convinced. For when the individual sacrifices himself, there is involved a lack of equality and instead of gaining, the relationship loses any validity it ever had. If Damayanti were to sacrifice Mohan to her father, she would have certain subtler satisfactions which would corrupt her personal life:

> Every day you have the insidious pleasure of seeing the Rajah, a man of great intelligence and charm, turning himself into a child before you.

And, to compensate herself for the greater loss, she would demand more and more power:

> In order to render your existence endurable, in order to stifle your inward self-contempt, you would need every false support you could find. . . . What

of your private dealings with yourself? My child, I don't think you could stop your inner life from becoming an endless series of repressed irritations, feigned amiabilities, calculated generosities, and forced enthusiasms.

In any case the relationship with her father is a false one of dominator and dominated; her father has gradually turned himself into Damayanti's spoilt child. The Guru realises the difficulties Damayanti has to contend with—she is drawn in two directions and cannot reconcile the two forces; and so he brings his own past experience—of an aunt whom he had loved but from whose possessiveness he had needed to escape—to bear on the problem. He points out to Damayanti how our feelings often lie outside reason or control and how "one's emotions offer one no steady guidance, and their orders are often inconsistent with one another." What is needed in relationship is a humility that will enable both people to treat the other as an equal and with complete candour.

Conceit fastens your attention on to your father, while leaving your own character and happiness out of account—and incidentally Mohan's as well. Isn't there something rather suspect in this ostensible self-elimination?

Damayanti is in the grip of the "authority of old-established things and with all the sentiment that clings to them," and she must realise this; such authority is not a "Higher Authority to which she *ought* to give blind obedience." She must not give way to a false sense of duty, for those who do often do so from very mixed motives:

I am suspicious of duty because it has come to be associated with obedience to rules of conduct which have a social rather than a spiritual sanction. Duty, in other words, often offers an excuse for obeying the letter instead of the spirit of the law. And people often mistake the satisfaction which comes from conforming to public opinion and receiving the world's approval for the satisfaction of real right doing.

It is a poor sort of character, he points out, "that can find its pleasure in acting wrongly or in the self-conceit which springs from a grim, self-enforced right-doing." The Guru relates what he has been saying to spiritual laws, which he considers as potent in their sphere as material laws in theirs. And so Damayanti must talk to her father—and must fight against "the pessimism, the cynicism, that will attack [her] in the semblance of pity"; she must realise her father is wrong and that unhappiness and deterioration of character will follow if she gives way. The drag of the past is to be feared; it affords its experience, of course, but it tends towards

repetitions, stagnation, and peace—peace of fidelity to tradition, of obedience to authority, peace which is really decay.

What faces Damayanti, in fact, if she accedes to her father is the sort of life represented by Bhoj and Lakshmi—the social life—which exists by crushing all real feelings. On the other hand the Guru does not spare her from forewarnings of the complexities of true relationship:

A close and equal relationship calls for patience, candour, and great sacrifices of pride. No longer will you be able to keep a private chamber from which, solitarily, to direct your relations with the loved one. No! Your will must exercise itself solely in keeping that chamber open to him. This is internal self-surrender, which is humility, instead of external self-sacrifice, which is pride.

It implies great "anxiety and effort—the effort of constantly rejecting the letter of the law and reasserting the spirit—this involves a constant dying accompanied by a constant re-birth. It is necessary to have faith—faith in the future."

Damayanti follows the Guru's teaching; she and Mohan are married; but their troubles are not over. The relationship is treated with a profound unsentimentality; the implications of the Guru's advice have still to be worked out. Difficulties, as in all human relationships, arise, and arise on the basis which the Guru has suggested—that of dominance and of submission. Damayanti, fond of dominating, tends to ignore Mohan; Mohan on his side refuses to face his problems with all the depth of his nature:

No matter how earnestly Mohan began, a temperamental distaste for exploring beneath the surface of things would soon cause him to swerve aside into flippancy.

A time comes when Mohan avoids Damayanti; he is becoming frustrated, and will takes the place of spontaneity. He thinks his efforts to improve the peasants are failing; what, he wonders, are Damayanti and he but "a pair of clowns." The father once more enters Damayanti's life; there are quarrels and reconciliations; but a tension is created, and, hence, a failure in the relationship. Once more the Guru points to the cause:

Mohan is holding himself apart from the peasants in an attempt to 'manage' them just as you are holding yourself apart in an attempt to manage Mohan.

Damayanti has been hiding her true feelings; Mohan must be told them whether he wants to hear or not:

If he does not want to, it is because he has his own private reasons, which are not good ones, for ignoring the truth. The person from whom knowledge is kept or truth is withheld is nearly always at fault. . . . Children cling to their childishness, aristocrats to the accepted notion of aristocratic nature, soldiers to the accepted notion of soldierliness, and so on—all for the sake of the advantages they gain by being incomplete human beings.

Damayanti is wrong in clinging to the "typical prerogatives of the typical Woman."

A temporary reconciliation follows, but it is incomplete. The influence of the past is still a factor to be reckoned with; it comes to be represented by the persons of Bhoj and Lakshmi. Damayanti becomes intimate with Lakshmi, and the two women indulge in frequent bouts of self-congratulation tinged with self-pity:

After a long talk in which they had both been filled with a melancholy but not unpleasurable sense of the tragic beauty of their lives . . .

though Damayanti soon comes to look on this relationship with a sardonic eye.

Mohan and Damayanti remain, then, apart; quarrels do no good. Mohan revolts against his wife's overbearing ways; he sees that Bhoj is in Lakshmi's toils and he wishes to escape such feminine domination. He discovers that Damayanti has been using private money to cover up failures and deficiencies in their common undertaking and this brings things to a head. But when a complete rupture seems inevitable, a letter from the Guru causes a certain re-consideration. Faced with the prospect of seeing the Guru, who reproaches them for staying away, they are at a loss what to say: "We must think," says Mohan. "We!" —he had said "We!" Damayanti breaks down and the two come together again.

The reconciliation that follows provides a scene of admirable restraint. The outcome is not a feeling of exaltation but a change of being, a sense of "something being given up";

Each had given up the same thing; each was weary with the same weariness, consoled with the same consolation, and above all thankful with the same thankfulness.

They decide that their new home shall be by the pool of Vishnu.

Such is the story of Mohan and Damayanti, and such the basis of that personal life which Myers would substitute for the dominative-submissive relationship which he felt to be so profoundly wrong. The story is not without its faults—it is rather long, it lacks climax and flows too evenly. Nevertheless it is a profound analysis of certain aspects of human intercourse.

What is implied by Myers's conception of Personal Relationships might well be summarised before its possible modes of application are considered. There must, he believes, be a complete equality between persons entering into relationship; and the relationship itself must be the result of the spontaneous movement of the heart, of what the individual really wants to do and not of a sense of social duty. The past is suspect, and too great an attention to its traditions can lead to a deadening of new responses to particular situations; these involve the necessity of a continual re-birth of the personality. There is, however, also a negative side. Damayanti has to reject her father in order to accept Mohan. Nothing is made easy—the continual newness of response involves spiritual effort. A person has a *personal* worth which is quite different from his social status (Myers does not believe with some marxists that all men are completely conditioned by society), and so the individual can choose on a *personal* basis. Finally the sense of the ultimate oneness of human existence provides Myers with his idea of the Centre: "all communion is through the Centre. When the relation of man with man is not through the Centre, it corrupts and destroys itself." Human relationships, that is to say, must recognise and respect the divine essence that is in every *person*. It is this that forms the basis for the absolute equality of all persons and that necessitates complete frankness as between person and person. The Centre symbolises the divine spiritual union of mankind.

The wider repercussions of these ideas as seen in *The Pool of Vishnu* must now be examined. In this book, as opposed even to *The Root and the Flower*, we are in touch with the mass of mankind, though only to a superficial extent. In the background are war and the famished hordes of Indian peasants whom war has despoiled. The Gujans and the peasants with whom Mohan deals enter into the picture; Mohan's trick of lining the road with dead peasants to draw attention to their wants and the Guru's mention of Nerodi Das, the poor man, in order to move the heart of Akbar on the peasants' behalf, serve to make us mindful of

the heaving and straining of these multitudes that seemed to build up huge, half-conscious demi-urges driving the world forward on a dark tortuous way.

The responsibility of the individual towards the rest of mankind is stressed. The Guru visits the Emperor on behalf of the peasants; Mohan looks upon them as "his children" and the efforts of the two, in contrast to the social irresponsibility of the palace inhabitants, are towards helping them; Myers feels that only the dispossessed Mohan was likely to care for the peasants—those in authority bother little.

These notions spring from Myers's belief in essential goodness and his idea that we should attempt to build on our common humanity—that individual people are basically fine and that only the social order is corrupt. "By nature and instinct," says the Guru, "persons are friends." He expresses his feeling on the matter to Jali:

It now seems to me like this: if one sees a man struggling at the bottom of a well, one is moved to do all one can to pull him out. If a man is starving, one's natural impulse is to share one's food with him. Surely it is only on second thoughts that people don't do these things? Society seems to me to be like an organised system of rather mean, second thoughts. In theory, no doubt, society helps men to help one another, but actually, it provides every man with arguments for helping himself and not helping others.

And so, the personal basis of human relationship is to be applied to vast matters of imperial policy. The 'typical' is the enemy; the body or mass is crude and monstrous and,

behind these monsters there is not the power of Spirit. Spirit in its human manifestation resides in persons, and that is why the personal is also universal. The popular leader, the subtle statesman or lawyer—they speak only for the monster of the day, and their words die. But the man who speaks out of his own personal depths speaks for all men, is heard by all men, and his words do not die. His is the voice of Spirit, by virtue of which humanity is eternally one.

When a man surrenders to the typical, he joins a small artificial body of men, entering into contact with them on a superficial level in order to lead a shallow life. He is afraid of entering into contact with humanity, which can only be reached upon a deep level—the level of the personal life.

When the Guru goes to see Akbar, it is on this basis that he appeals to the Emperor. He tells Jali how at the first meeting he longed to point out to Akbar the unreality of the scene of court life around him and how easy an understanding with Salim would be:

Every action is personal at its roots. If Akbar talks to me about the succession I shall be obliged to treat this great, public question as a small, personal question, and that, indeed, it is.

He points out how little of 'history' touches the multitudes who are nevertheless dragged into the fray; and in the end he considers that the element of make-believe will destroy the respect for 'history' that people may have. Yet he feels hopeful about Akbar because, being born in Islam, Akbar believes instinctively that all men are equal. There is no hierarchy, no priestly caste there—"nothing to stand between men and God." Greatness, of which, perhaps, Akbar has a sort, comes from *inside* and is not something conferred externally by society. "Human conventions and institutions he values at no more than their true worth."

And so the Guru, after a false start, ("True feeling was absent and I tried to replace it by cleverness") speaks to Akbar from his heart and tells a story of Nerodi Das, a peasant, of his "increasing struggle against starvation." And, as we have seen, he gets his edict for the peasants.

The other point to be remembered is that Myers has a rare appreciation of individual worth and of the need for individual action; although all Spirit is one, yet "by an unalterable rhythm of our being we swing out from the world of communion into the world of separated things." One remembers Gokal's desire not to intrude on Amar—and Amar's dislike of oppressiveness in other people. Mohan and Damayanti strive towards 'community', but they do so nevertheless only because they independently and individually wish to do so spontaneously and from the heart of their being. "We go forth, we meet, and in the meeting we are as one. At one also with all life." The difficulty that Jali puts forward "How—in the world of separation—to hold fast?" gets its answer:

One must cling to the memory. One must remember and one must act. The knowledge gained in communion, and ripened in solitude, must pour its life into the world through action.

If a man withdraws for selfish reasons, he is lost. But if it is to "concentrate his powers and achieve his soul's unity," then his withdrawal is good:

Into loneliness the spirit by its nature swings; and, as it is only in communion and action that man learns, so it is only in loneliness that he discovers what he has learnt. Nevertheless from his solitude—yes, and from communion!—man must always return.

Thus there must be both 'togetherness' and 'apartness'; and togetherness can only be truly based on individual integrity, not on submission to an external common code. Man finds his togetherness only through an apprehension of Spirit in the universe, in fact, through the Centre. Spirit is the world's master:

You know that you are not the slave of mechanical fate, but the master of divine destiny. You know that there is a divine meaning in the life of the world —in the life of men, of you, and of me.

One more feature of the Guru's political conception is seen in his speech with Mobarek. The Shaik who represents much that Myers dislikes, finds himself unable to accept Akbar's new edicts and, in talking with the Guru, points to his own hierarchical conception of society. The State is to determine temporal duties; he has introduced into India

the Church [as] an institution by means of which man can satisfy—in the religious sphere—his desire for order, his respect for tradition, his craving for continuity. Church and State! On these I base the whole edifice of Society, Civilization, Culture.

He stands by "the traditions, the institutions, and observances" which enshrine the "deep wisdom, the sacred wisdom" that man is privileged to inherit; and it is in Society as at present constituted—"in its traditions, its institutions—nay in its very structure—that we discern most clearly the guiding hand of God." And so "the higher creature must discharge the higher function." The Shaik provides the rational argument for the pre-eminence of such people as Bhoj; for by 'higher' creature he intends the higher born. The multitude become mere units of work and effort, and it is the statesmen's task to direct them for the common good.

To this the Guru puts forward his ideas:

My theories . . . amount to nothing more than that every man has the right to be treated as a person . . . and not merely as a member of a category or class.

For our common human nature holds the seeds of wisdom: "In a sense we are all born to wisdom. I mean as a child is wise." Certainly we need experience to develop it; but the point is that:

Each man must find his own. The wisdom of another is not *my* wisdom, just as his goodness is not *my* goodness. And only my wisdom and my goodness are going to work my salvation Neither the one nor the other can be imposed.

This does not mean that tradition is to be ignored—provided that

the words strike into me as true. When from among the dead someone addresses me and I enter into relation with him, then it is as though a friend walked by my side.

But the type of tradition of which Mobarek speaks the Guru stigmatises as a "mound of corpses." It is impossible to discover the "higher creature in the higher functions." "The highest that we know are equally within the range of all men." Yet not all are equally worthy; there is a "very pernicious kind of tolerance—I mean a refusal to condemn wicked and foolish views." (The criteria for rejection are not, however, revealed.) Compromise is possible but not adulteration. "A terrible purity of intention is demanded of man." Not to trust human nature means that Government must depend on lies; and thus the Guru condemns Mobarek's conception:

"No!" returned the Guru in a voice that had become stern. "There is no greatness at the end of your road—only despair. Spirit, which must stream through the individual man, if he is to preserve a sane and living soul, must stream through society as well. Every civilization, every culture, that has ever existed has owed its life to this. When the stream tarries the body politic stiffens into a prison-house; forms and institutions become manacles, and the State turns into a monstrous slave-driver. . . . The leaders will tell you that they are acting under divine inspiration, or that they are obeying inexorable laws; and always they will dangle before the multitude the vulgar emblems of an impossible glory. But there is death in their hearts."

And so the type of society which Myers ultimately recommends is that of Mohan and Damayanti, at Hawa Ghar,—the type that Jali discovers in his adventures through the book:

Here at Hawa Ghar there was a correspondence between outward things and the inner landscapes of the mind. . . . He had a sense of security; he saw the complications of the world as artificialities painted over the true forms of life. And the contemplation of those forms brought comfort.

For at the centre of this book is the pool of Vishnu; even if the Guru dies, Vishnu remains.

The book closes with the young prince once more on the balcony of the Old Palace at Agra, where he had stood as a child at the beginning. The wheel has come full circle; the near and the far have met, there is a complete correspondence between inner desire and outward manifestation; society and individual meet in balanced harmony; the education of Jali is complete.

Myers obviously intended the ideas of the Guru to have a relevance beyond the immediate concerns of a couple of characters in the book. To this extent, at least, *The Pool of Vishnu* is a vehicle for the promulgation of certain notions about human behaviour, in a way that is not true of the other books. "Every action," Myers believes, "is personal at its roots." What he is against is an approach to life, pervasive throughout our present-day society, that clings to 'things', whatever those things may be—position, power, money—in preference to the acknowledgement of 'persons', of humanity. Or, to employ Buber's terminology, the 'world of it' in preference to the 'world of thou'. As Myers reveals in the Preface to *The Pool of Vishnu*, Buber's work—*I and Thou*—expresses much of his own thought on these matters. The essence of Buber's idea lies in the fact that when "Thou" is spoken, the speaker enters into a relation involving what may be termed reciprocal obligations, although the word "obligation" suggests perhaps something set down, fixed, and stereotyped that is foreign to Buber's purpose; for in Buber's conception, as to a less degree in Myers's, "The primary word I—Thou can be spoken only with the whole being"; the implications of the sentence "All real living is meeting," lie behind Buber's conception; and "relation is mutual"—love, in fact, is responsibility of an 'I' for a 'Thou'.

In Myers's exposition there is, as we have seen, no facile emotionalism. The type of relationship that he seeks to represent through Mohan and Damayanti is one which, it is felt, can be respected, even if one feels that the situation involves some simplification and ignores certain aspects of human nature which ought, perhaps, to have greater prominence. This feeling has been admirably expressed by a great admirer of Myers's novels, who wrote to him when the novel was in typescript:

I find a want of unity between the Story and the Story-Teller which, I think, is due to the impression I get of passivity in 29 chapters—19 concerning Jali and

10 concerning Mohan and Damayanti. Read your own introduction to *The Root and the Flower*. There you will find the significant comment: "What one ignores one is apt to forget." The Story-Teller ignores that however deeply human beings may *think* of themselves in relation to the universe they *feel* much more deeply the conflict between the senses and the intellect, between the physical and the spiritual. . . . The Story-Teller as a connoisseur in character uses his characters almost as actors in a Morality Play—they express ambition—jealousy — courage — greed — vanity — selfishness — pride — pity — cruelty —but the Story-Teller appears deliberately to ignore one of the most profound of human needs and most powerful of influences. Sex instinct may be quiescent, but it is still rich and unruly *life*; but the Story-Teller almost entirely denies to his important characters this means by which they may acquire the gift of moral and spiritual experience which is that particular experience of sex when passion is the outward and visible expression of an inward and spiritual consummation and creates the only real "*equal* relationship" between man and woman. . . . [In the relationship of Mohan and Damayanti] the omission appears to be intentional and deliberate because in the struggle between her love for Mohan and her Father no *desire* for Mohan adds any weight in the scales towards a decision in Mohan's favour.

Although the Story-Teller insists on the value of candour and there is much "argument about it and about," in all the conversations there is no deep intimacy, no true exchange of real wishes, or of vital experience, or secret knowledge of life.

To this Myers replied (3 May 1939) in terms which will help to clarify his position as a writer of philosophical novels:

Your letter is very interesting and I am certainly grateful to you for taking the trouble to express your views. Your warning is to be taken seriously: I'm sure of that. But I'm not sure that I can—or want to—do more about it than avoid flatness and propagandism. One can't write about what doesn't interest one, so it would be useless my trying to introduce sex or passion or romance more freely; nor do I really think I need to in *this* volume, for the first one has dealt with all that sufficiently it seems to me; and I want my reader to move on with me to other interests. But I don't want to be flat or schoolmasterish; and surely I ought to be able to avoid that. I must try in the last Part (Part VII which is unwritten) to be less detached—less "*passive*" you would say. But I don't quite understand your word "passivity." I am intensely *interested* myself in the ethical and sociological ideas that are the undercurrent, and I ought to be able to communicate my interest to my reader. The only criticism you make which I can't agree to is that I don't give any "true exchange of real wishes or of vital experience or secret knowledge of life." It seems to me that I do do this—at any rate much more than in *The Root and the Flower*. I am certainly tapping a deeper and maturer layer of myself in this last book. Well, well!—I will continue to ponder your remarks. And I have intended—and do now intend still more—to be less detached in the concluding part of the book.

Yet, despite Myers's defence of his method, one feels the force of the writer's criticism, bearing in mind the peculiarities of her idiom. Once more the style of this volume is admirably clear and lucid, limpid and easy-flowing. But for all its 'positiveness' it still lacks nervous strength. The passivity the writer notes is as much a feature of the style as of the incidents. The 'spirit of place' that Lawrence had so profoundly is beyond the scope of Myers; and, as a further contrast, it is interesting to note that Lawrence's descriptions usually stress movement, a sense of life behind the most tranquil setting, a hidden dynamism as it were, which Myers was never able to *suggest*. Even in those scenes of tranquillity which he depicts so frequently, the essence of stillness is not caught. He was never interested in his descriptions; and despite the praise they have received they all too often become little more than backcloths.

These weaknesses are partly due to the possession of a mind which, for all its anti-intellectualism, was as has been stressed, primarily analytical by nature. The notion of personal relationships is too intellectualised to recommend itself to some minds. It exists, as the writer above hints at, on a basis of taking thought; the candour that comes in sex experience, when the body speaks, is lacking. And inevitably, the intense vitality of the destructive ego is lost sight of, an omission that the belief in the 'natural' goodness of man encourages. Society is a poor substitute for the Devil as a producer of evil.

In the novel, it seems to me, Myers's great weakness, and an important one for a writer so concerned with the problem of personal relationships, is his inability really to convey the impact of character on character. We never really seem to be given the to-and-fro of relationship in direct physio-psychological contact; the sheer 'nerves' of relationship, which Lawrence conveys so marvellously, are lacking. It is significant that out of the tetralogy the characters one experiences most fully are Amar, part of the essence of whose character is the hard element of coldness, and the young Jali in his isolation; it is as if Myers was best able, in the last resort, to depict those who like himself had to a certain degree detached themselves from other people. The split, suggested by the writer quoted above, between the sexual, passional and the intellectual, analytical, self is perhaps the fundamental reason why Myers fails to enter the ranks of the very greatest writers. There are moments when one feels that, despite his constant criticism of people for assuming masks with which to face the world—masks which hid real personality as well as revealed assumed characteristics—he hid from his conscious self certain aspects of the sexual life, to which he himself was a prey and with which he could not come to terms. Certainly in the last resort he does not make the emotional and the intellectual life into a coherent whole; there is a hint of the 'doggish' in his attitude to sex—

as in Hari, hanging about 'on heat'. One wonders, indeed, if in this matter one cannot apply to Myers something of that ironic comment which he makes against Ali in *The Root and the Flower*—

> Granted that Ali had an inborn instinct to shut his eyes and turn away from all knowledge that was inconvenient, did that make him a fool? If Ali had the art of avoiding experiences that were likely to teach him what he didn't want to know, was he the less intelligent for that? If he used his counterfeit knowledge of the world as a protection against deeper understanding, if his pretensions were primarily of service in deceiving himself, was that attitude necessarily a stupid one?

For, surely, one detects in *The Pool of Vishnu* something more than a loss of 'interest' in sex; the avoidance is too significant in a book so explicitly concerned with inter-sex relationship and it may spring from a general decline in vitality—which other features of the book bear out—or a subconscious avoidance of a painful topic, or most likely, a mixture of the two.

To be fair to Myers, he was not unaware of the danger of over-simplification—that his interests might make the view of human nature he was giving in *The Pool of Vishnu* too unsubtle to convey the infinite complexity of human nature; and when the father of Mr Walter Allen pointed something of this out to him, he signified the justice of the criticism:

> Your father has put his finger straight on a great mistake of mine in my book —a mistake made from hurry and impatient weariness in the last weeks of work on it. I had intended to make the Guru soliloquize, or say to Jali or Damayanti: "The universe and human beings are not so simple as I have made out. I am aware of this. I have forced the universe into a narrow world for the sake of emphasizing certain aspects of it." Then I wondered whether it would not be better not to give the Guru this vision, but to let it be seen that I, the author, did not consider that the Guru had said the last word. But, finally, in my hurry to be finished I just *forgot* about all this. I much regret it now, because I do appear to think I have approached much nearer to the heart of things than I have ever really believed—even in my most conceited moments.
> If you have read Jung's last book (but I can't understand how you and your father ever have time to read at all!) and if I tell you that I have read all of Jung, you will see that I can hardly fail to be painfully aware of my mistake—and you will perhaps wonder how I came to make it.
> The answer lies partly, perhaps, in this: That one can't do different things at the same time. I could, and ought, however, to have avoided laying myself open to one part of your father's just criticism (2 Aug. 1940).

But he also realised the necessity of taking a stand on his faith and that what might be termed the propagandist element in his work was not something to be deprecated but an essential part of a legitimate purpose, even if that purpose is not primarily that of a novelist. Thus he continues in the same letter:

Where I think I do not agree with your father is in his apparent unwillingness to say of any one faith this is better or truer than that. And again that one should never 'impose' one way of thought. 'Impose' no! But persuade, yes. And not by deeds alone. By words as well. In my own experience I have been profoundly enlightened by words, by ideas, spoken or in books. I do think that your father is now perhaps going too far—not in acceptance of the Whole—but in acceptance of good and evil alike because they are parts of the Whole. While recognizing the mysterious necessity of evil and its part in producing good, one must, it seems to me, go on hating it and even "condemning" it. For it is not good to be above good and evil—even out of wisdom.

Alas! all this and more I had to leave out of my book. I hadn't *time*.

Yet, despite this simplification, Myers's notion introduces an important and vital element in human relationships at the level of self-consciousness. Oddly enough, despite his distrust of duty, his idea works in terms of the *will* rather than of instinct. Its centrifugal egotistic notion of the 'spontaneous' self, what one wants to do, is balanced by the need to *respect* the other person. "Effort" is needed. Myers, of course, was never so naïve as to imagine that his ideas would achieve immediate or sudden resolution. He makes Mohan and Damayanti realise that failure in community is practically inevitable for mankind:

She [Damayanti] smiled.
"The world is not going to change in a day."
"All the same, you and Mohan are changing a little bit of it."
"Not even that," she shook her head. "I mean, not permanently. This attempt of ours is bound to end in failure."
"Why?"
"Because it is, in a sense, premature. But that doesn't mean that the attempt ought not to be made. People must go on making attempts. Otherwise there will never be any change at all."

As I have said above, it is not unfair to treat Myers's ideas as having a practical application, for much of the driving force behind his work was hortatory, and his profoundly ethical interests make it not unjust to believe that not only did he desire to display human conduct but also to influence that of his readers. All profound works of art require of the reader a readjustment of personality in the light of insight obtained: and that insight in one way or another must in the end alter, or at least influence, conduct. If Myers's ideas are a little more direct in their application—if as one reads one is aware of a pragmatic purpose—that is not necessarily to be taken as a condemnation of his work though it may lessen his stature as a novelist: yet poetry, as Matthew Arnold says, is "at bottom a criticism of life," and the reader who refuses to recognise the 'practical' (certain connotations of word 'practical' are perhaps un-fortunate, but it is difficult to think of a better word) application of artistic creation may be guilty of erecting that "private heaven" for aesthetes that I. A. Richards has condemned, or of partaking of that "rather petty form of aestheticism" which Myers himself repudiated.

Yet it is difficult to see that the type of solution that Myers has pro-pounded has any very great *practical* application to the present-day tensions of society. It would not be completely untrue to state that in certain important respects, Myers's work is anachronistic; for, in some ways, he is the last of the Victorians. Fundamentally he is an aristocrat, and even the type of personal relationships that he recommends is one that is only possible within a small, highly intelligent, self-conscious, and, perhaps, leisured class. For, of course, one's conception of personal relationships is ultimately bound up with one's conception of oneself, and is socially conditioned though to a lesser degree than the attitudes of the Maynes, the Walter Standishes and the Daniyals of this world. Ulti-mately, the dichotomy of man and society is a false one. The relation-ship of Mohan and Damayanti is the product not, as Myers would have us believe, of a purely spontaneous feeling, but of a more deliberately conditioned refinement, plus, of course, a natural inborn sensitivity. Before one can treat a person as a person, in Myers's conception of that word, one has to have gathered one's conception of personality from somewhere, and that somewhere must be chiefly the society around one tempered by individual sensitivity. Myers's own rejection of people like Daniyal may well spring from the greater intellectual and emotion-al fastidiousness that formed part of his own nature in conjunction with the seriousness of his upbringing at Leckhampton House.

Again, to "build on our common humanity" is not as easy as it sounds; nor, to do Myers justice, (as we have seen) does he hide the difficulty. Common humanity hides uncommon divergence, and it seems to me that difference in degree can be so profound that it emerges as a difference in type. Those whose life-experience has been different from Myers's can get much from him; but at a time when so much emphasis is being placed on the fundamental similarity of men, it may well be advisable to draw attention to the enormously wide divergence of types to be found—a divergence, incidentally, that is pervasive throughout Myers's own work, so that he himself admits the necessity for rejection. Many classes of society have undergone too different a type of life from that of Myers himself, for any easy acceptance of what he has to say; their emotional outlook is too bound up with the tensions of twentieth-century existence, to accept any great change of heart (Myers of course, belongs to the Yogi rather than to the Commissar class, to use Koestler's useful division). Few people attain the necessary degree of detachment and self-consciousness that Myers himself exhibited. That is not to say that it is not possible to work out a personal solution on a purely instinctive level—many people do, and there is more of what might be termed 'natural' goodness in the world than a certain modern type of intellectual is prepared to admit. But the dynamics of social power rarely permit such people to gain positions of authority; and, in any case, the handling of groups and of group relationships demands a different, and usually a morally lower, approach than the one which Myers advocates. The exercise of power, for which it would hardly be possible to deny the necessity, is a much more complicated thing than Myers suggests; and a degree of impersonality, in a large-scale community such as we have to-day, is unavoidable—and indeed, not without its value, provided that impersonality is guided by notions of right and justice, notions which in any case must inevitably enter even into the most purely personal relationship. For, even in the 'I—Thou' communion, the abstract world must play a part. It is difficult to see, for instance, how it is possible to put the relationship of Akbar and his own son *purely* on a personal basis, as the Guru suggests. The fate of the Empire must enter as a consideration.[1]

Again, Myers in his condemnation of institutional life, of the hierarchical conception of society and of order, seems to blind himself to the liberating aspect of the order and discipline that such a conception *could* involve. To recognise superiority in one's fellow men seems to involve as much a tribute to the divine essence in man as to act always on a basis of equality does; at least it is necessary to distinguish between different sorts of equality. What is wrong is the recognition of the wrong type of superiority—a superiority based on money, or dead tradition, etc.—that was what Myers was, fundamentally, condemning, for it is impossible to ignore the profoundly aristocratic nature of his work. As T. E. Hulme has expressed it: "Order is not merely negative, but creative and liberating. Institutions are necessary." To regard life purely on a 'personal' basis, therefore, seems to leave out certain aspects of human existence which are not without their value amidst the imperfections of this world.

Yet the very positiveness of Myers's approach acts as an incentive in a world that has produced so vast a volume of destructive criticism but has found few to offer positive solutions. In its way the final effect of the book is to affect a certain sense of emotional liberation. Moreover

[1] Very relevant to their whole discussion of the 'personal' is Lawrence's rejection of the contemporary emphasis on 'personality' and the 'personal'; he writes in a letter to Katherine Mansfield: "I want some new non-personal activity which is at the same time a genuine vital activity. And I want relations which are not purely personal, based on purely personal qualities; but relations based on some unanimous accord in truth or belief, and a harmony of *purpose*, other than of personality."

to point to restriction is not to deny importance but merely to define significance more closely. The emphasis laid on personal relationships is obviously a vital one for the individual; and the whole analysis of existing society, with Myers's capacity to relate apparently disparate aspects of social existence, is an achievement of the first order. The social types he analyses he knows intimately. His novels enlarge one's understanding of the workings of certain sorts of mind and reproduce with remarkable fidelity the moral effects of attempting to live up to standards that have lost their validity. His concern for qualitative considerations in relationship would, alone, lend importance to his work. His theme, ultimately, is very similar to that of Henry James. He looks for the "free play of intelligence" as opposed to the aridity which is all that comes from the fundamentally conventional existence, for the freedom to express the self's deepest nature, to live, in Isabel Archer's terms, the "personal life,"[1] untrammelled by one's consciousness of the effect one is making on others, expresses one of the deepest themes of both writers and, at the same time, points to an element without which both consider the truly civilised life impossible.

[1] Cf. *The Portrait of a Lady* by Henry James.

CHAPTER V

"STRANGE GLORY"

S *trange Glory* is the shortest of Myers's books. Coming between *The Root and the Flower* and *The Pool of Vishnu*, it is the most romantic of his works and reveals more clearly, perhaps, than any of his others the strain of mysticism in him. It deals more explicitly with those transcendental standards by which our earthly desires are to be judged and in terms of which our human relationships take on significance. For once more, relationship is the central theme of the novel—though this time the theme is explored not in a social milieu but in direct contact with the earth and the timelessness of forest and swamp. Myers's own attitude is precipitated through two of the characters, Stephen and Tom Wentworth. The novel is written from the point of view of a third person, however, Paulina; and Paulina is another Jali in the sense that Myers explores, through the relationships of Paulina and Jali with other people, the possibilities of right human conduct. Paulina, however, exists much more than was the case with Jali in the feelings than the intellect. She wishes to achieve right personal relationships, but the social scene and the corruption of society play a less notable part—perhaps because at this stage of Myers's life the 'dream' element is predominant and the pull of social conventions seems momentarily—only momentarily—less potent.

When the novel opens, Paulina, a very rich young woman, is visiting a portion of the Louisiana swamps during a stay at Pontchartrain. She comes into momentary conversation with a man who is sitting on a fallen tree-trunk, watching her. Exactly a year later, she returns to the same spot, and, once again meeting the same stranger, Tom Wentworth, is taken to his house. Charmed with the spot, she decides to buy the piece of land on which it stands and which is for sale, despite a fear of ridicule from her mother, and from Mr Berkeley Pell, who looks after her immense fortune. This brings her into further contact with the hermit, as she calls the stranger. Her marriage to Harry, Lord Bridgnorth, follows soon after, despite a warning from Wentworth. The marriage is a failure and she seeks more and more the companionship of the swamp and of Wentworth, although, in fact, he turns out to be a man who has killed her uncle.

The years pass, and her friendship with Wentworth continues. It is at his house in the forest that she meets Stephen. The rest of the book is taken up with her relationship to the two men. Stephen is a young scientist with whom she falls in love physically; her relationship with Wentworth remains platonic. Stephen is married; his wife lives in Russia—she is actually Wentworth's daughter, Caroline. And at the end of the novel Stephen is recalled to Russia. Paulina prepares to follow him after the death of Wentworth, who has fallen ill with an incurable disease and whom she has stayed behind to nurse. Just before she leaves, a letter arrives to say that Stephen and Caroline are dead. However, their little son, Matthew, survives. Paulina goes to join him.

In the first part, the heroine is shown to be torn between two worlds; one is that of society represented by her mother, her lover Rupert, a very shadowy figure, and Mr Berkeley Pell; the economic crisis of 1931 exists in the background. The other is that of the timeless forest and swamp whose inhabitants represent higher human aspirations of love and the mystical. At the beginning, Paulina has encountered the Louisiana swamp for the first time—"an elegant young lady," in the stillness and silence. It is perhaps significant that at first the swamp is connected with decay—the trees "half killed by the grey moss that hung on beards from every branch. It was like old age. And whole forests were dying from it. Dying forests! Windless air! Grey-bearded age! And silence—always silence!" Paulina feels herself a *ghost*.

At first her feeling for the forest is vague and diffuse; a romantic indulgence rather than a clearly defined sympathy, a means to integration. "Didn't she feel empty enough, bodiless enough, vague and distant and melancholy enough, to be one [a ghost]." When she leaves, she is still in a dream. The vulgar whine of a pleasure boat brings her back again to the realities of social life—to the young men and women in the streets—and Rupert, her lover ("Damn Rupert") and the physical beauty of her figure. Thus the stage is set: the values of the forest, as yet superficial, manifested only as an indulgence in romantic and vague sentiment, over against the values of the steam-boat, pleasure, social obligation, Rupert, the body—in a word, society.

This division is fundamental for understanding the book, though actual social analysis, as I have indicated, plays little part. In the first section the scales are held fairly equal and the theme is developed in various subtle ways. Society it is, of course, that gradually becomes unreal and the forest real. With the passage of time Rupert disappears from the scene and her love of him becomes "a shadow." Pauline realises that what she wants are

enduring things . . . dependable things. I want dependableness in myself—I don't want only appearances of sameness—like the smells, and the business, and the damp Pontchartrain air.—I want things that are the same to themselves—persons, I suppose—and I want to be the same to myself and to them.

This dependability—this search for an integration that will lend her stability of purpose—she pursues in the swamp forest and in her relationship with the stranger she meets there.

But the forest and the stranger are not to be regarded as agencies through which she can escape from responsibility. In time they bring their own deeper and more creative demands. Paulina wishes to linger in the forest—but she also wants to take roots; and to take root implies growth.

Her first act is to buy the piece of forest on which Wentworth's house is built. The worlds of Mr Berkeley Pell and of the stranger are thus brought into explicit contact. The buying of the forest constitutes, symbolically, an act of defiance to the whole propertied world. The portrait of Mr Pell, the financier, is one of the few satiric, ironic portraits in Myers. In a number of touches (the ironically awed method of treatment, the absurdly hierophantic atmosphere surrounding the banker) the absurdity of the financial world is exposed. Money is death, and when Paulina goes to the vaults to fetch her bonds she thinks of "the catacombs in Rome, and the tombs of the Kings of Luxor."

Gradually Paulina is weaned from her unsuccessful social life. Her marriage to Harry, Lord Bridgnorth, is a failure, as Wentworth has warned her it would be. Harry attempts to break the connection between Paulina and Wentworth, whom she continues to visit year after year, by revealing that Wentworth has murdered Paulina's uncle, but he fails. By the end of the first part of the book the issue is becoming clearer.

The values of the forest stand over against those of society. Harry represents the latter; their marriage is based only on a superficial conventionality rather than on a profound community of interest. It is noticeable that the story tends to move more through incident than through direct analysis of social types. The positions of Harry, Paulina, and Wentworth are conveyed through action and dialogue. The social success and the outcast are shown in opposition; Stephen, believing in the new social order, is to be the bridge between them.

The next section is concerned with Paulina's growing intimacy with Tom and his son-in-law, Stephen. Now divorced, she is oppressed by a sense of failure; and so she seeks once more the healing 'silence' of the forest. It is on this occasion, eight years after her first meeting with Wentworth, that she first comes into contact with Stephen, who is staying with Tom. To Wentworth she explains the divorce: "Harry is very conventional . . . He clings to the old social order and to his privileges"—and, apparently, insisted on Paulina's thinking it a very fine order, too. And so the crash has come.

Paulina takes up her abode temporarily in Tom's house, and seems willing to abandon herself to the solitude of the bayou and its beauty; but Stephen prevents this retreat from direct personal life. He falls in love with her. The affair marks the challenge of life as Myers understood it at its finest, the challenge of an intimate, deep personal relationship:

But now all her peaceful thoughts were put to flight. Stephen's words dragged her back into the world where there was no serenity, a world of which she was weary.

The values of personal life, then, reassert themselves. As he waits for her at what is to be their first dinner together, Stephen considers the difference between Lady Bridgnorth and Paulina, between the social creature and the true person. Paulina in the meantime has been preparing herself for the meeting by making enquiries about Stephen from one of his colleagues. The young man, she discovers, is an eminent scientist and a Communist. When they meet, she shows at first a superficial social hardness, and Stephen is chilled. "There is Lady Bridgnorth speaking," he considers. Gradually, however, self-consciousness vanishes. A relationship between persons begins to emerge. Yet Stephen remains confused and anxious:

"But there," he reflected, "people were dancing, drinking, and making love —and doing so all the more furiously for being filled with anxiety or despair." . . . Then his thoughts went out to the little house in the forest. The beautiful, remote calm of death was a devastating criticism upon the petty, complicated, frustrated act of living. And yet Tom, who was now living right under the shadow of death, still rendered to life a simple and eager allegiance.

The two men obviously correspond to the two sides of Myers's nature—the social reformer and the mystic. On the one hand lies the reversion to simpler modes of being through contact with the eternities of nature; on the other the search for a new social philosophy that will lead to a juster social order, intimately bound up, as such a philosophy must be, with the question of right personal relationships.

What the two men stand for becomes increasingly explicit. At one of their meetings, Paulina asks Stephen to talk to her about Wentworth. Stephen explains that Wentworth is not a nature-worshipper, nor a dreamer; no one "has a livelier intellectual curiosity." The differences in their approach to scientific matters is dwelt on:

"I often complain that his interest in science is more romantic than scientific. I, as a hard-boiled scientist, believe in discovering truth, not inventing it. Tom retorts that science moves by the imagination, that logic itself rests upon intuition, and that facts are interesting only for the light they throw on the whole. His subjectivism seems to me to rest on scepticism; I call him cynical. He replies that my objectivism is cynical in another way—besides being at bottom naive."

9–24 pp.

Tom is not then to be regarded as an escapist. He does not dislike human beings individually, but social atmospheres. What he can best do is to follow his nature and his thoughts:

He believes that the ideal of self-illumination and the ideal of social duty are not incompatible, and that at his age what you think, and what you are, become more important than 'good works'.

Stephen agrees with Tom that in society

the sense of the brotherhood of men is almost completely lost. Society encourages the spirit of competitiveness and the cult of appearances.

He reveals himself to be a Communist because Communism sets out to form a society in which "each individual is *primus inter pares*." His actual experience of Russia has been disappointing. He finds himself unable to accept the "crudity of thought or bad manners." He admits that snobbishness, vanity, and pride have caused great advances in civilisation; but now he believes that

unless there comes a spiritual change, we shall be carried over a precipice.

Later, Paulina extends her understanding of Tom when she learns of his beliefs from his own mouth. In the forest, Wentworth explains, he gets the sense of the archetypal, not of the historic. He feels "particularly aware of the intertwining of our spiritual roots"—a feeling that comes to him from the earth, and from the swamp, which is "unlittered by the vestiges of human history." He believes in contact through individual relationship but also in a communion through the earth. In the forest he feels a sense of oneness with the life of the race and the ancestral life; there are millions of years of accumulated memories at the base of one's consciousness forming an earth-spirit which causes man's feeling for nature. Tom himself senses a curious cosmic intimacy—a communion with all life in the silence of the starry nights:

"There are certain nights in this forest," he went on, "when my sense of contact is quite extraordinarily strong—warm misty nights when the heavens are shut out and everything is still and near and intimate. And then there is quite another sort of experience that comes to me at times. It comes on nights like this, nights without either wind or mist or moon, nights when the stars are out. My spirit seems to project itself into the heavens so that the earth appears beneath me as a small solitary globe, and I obtain a particular sense of it as my home. I assure you that the love one then feels for the earth is intense; its composite spiritual entity is revealed and felt—and most curious and beautiful and varied it is."

He believes that men have a relationship with God but he comes "nearest to apprehending it by meditating on the eternal or archetypal forms." This is his answer to loneliness—in the forest one should not "feel it to

be indifferent or lifeless or alien . . . One cannot feel lonely or meaningless when one feels that one is a part of the life around one." In this
sense, the meaninglessness of both their marriages (for Tom's marriage,
too, has been a failure) convinces them of the need for a life of inner
significance. "The external life *is* meaningless, however busy and virtuous it is, unless it teaches you something."

Wentworth, then, stands for a mystical contact with life, a life on a
cosmic scale; it is Stephen who represents the individual relationship.
Wentworth says that Paulina means a great deal to him; but his relationship with her remains on the purely spiritual plane. Stephen, on the
other hand, seeks a much more physical contact. One of his meetings
with Paulina has not been satisfactory. He analyses the situation:

> Yesterday evening we were just ourselves. We gave no thought of our con-
> nexions with other people, our respective settings. . . . Each saw the other in
> freedom and isolation, and isn't that the way that human beings ought to come
> together? But this evening the world closed in round us.

Paulina, in fact, had "*wanted* to lose sight of" him, to "bury [him] under
entangling circumstances"; for women "are always servile to the world
and to circumstances." It is noticeable that his love for Paulina is presented in much more physical terms than is the case of Mohan and
Damayanti in *The Pool of Vishnu*. "He could not desist from recreating
in imagination the feel of her body against his while they were dancing."
There is more intimacy here than is customary in Myers's somewhat
intellectual studies of people, even if the situation is described in well-
worn terms.

The affair comes to a climax under the dominating influence of time.
It is noticeable that the relationship with Tom is measured in years;
that with Stephen in days. A crisis arises; Tom is found to be dying—
he can only live a few more months. Stephen discovers that it is not
possible to avoid the demands of social convention, that he must at any
rate temporarily return to Russia to his wife, and that Tom's claim on
Paulina's friendship during the few months he has to live, must be met.
He considers returning to America later, but realises that Matthew, his
child, may prove a difficulty; he does not know whether he will be able
to get him out of Russia.

All three therefore remain in a state of frustration and uncertainty.
Love, Paulina comes to realise, cannot be accepted without a struggle
and is something only to be snatched from out of the entangling circumstances. There is always, indeed, a certain frustrated quality about this
love story. Paulina senses the drag of the past:

> A longing for bygone things caught at her heart and that longing was joined
> by an intense craving for peace.

She feels the entangling circumstances of Stephen and his wife and child. Wentworth is faced by death and an uncertainty about the relationship of Stephen and Paulina—perhaps the subconscious jealousy that an older man has for a relationship which he cannot enjoy. Stephen is frustrated because he knows he must return to Russia and to the entanglements there.

Nevertheless, Paulina and Stephen accept their love in physical terms; for them it is to prove an eternal moment and such 'eternal moments' of pure relationship are important touchstones amidst the frustrations that love involves.

Thus the love affair with Stephen achieves, in a sense, its consummation. For a brief period they go away together. The whole situation, however, contains this element of tension—externally in the complex of relationships in which the lovers are involved, internally in Paulina's feeling of "being completely herself and true to herself," and at the same time having the feeling that she was "letting go, letting herself drift as passively as those detached water lily leaves that were drifting down stream." Her love brings her a sense of detachment, " 'This is another world', she thought, 'a far-away world that is like a world after death'." Yet it also brings a feeling of intensity and immediacy—she and outward things have passed:

How feeble and dilute was the sense of actuality that one got in ordinary life, how weak one's habitual apprehension of the wonder of the living Now.

For a moment, however, they have thrown off "the oppression of the past and the fear of the future." In doing so they have become as Gods. And for a period of ecstasy their feelings coalesce with the peace and silence of the setting:

Tender and mournful and strange did the fall of the night seem to Paulina as she lay on the still-warm deck. No lights burned in the little houses on the banks; there was no movement in all the silent landscape; the ragged outline of the trees against the sky was absolutely still.

There is a perfect harmony achieved between desire and fulfilment— though, as always in Myers, at the cost of a certain simplification and even of regression to simpler states of being.

When the revival of consciousness comes, after their return to Wentworth's hut, Paulina decides that even when Stephen has gone, there will be Tom—for "to leave Tom is unthinkable." The memory of Stephen, fraught as it will be with pain and folly, will have its secret shrine. The whole problem now resolves itself on the two planes of existence. There is the transcendental gospel according to Tom: "I want," he states fulness of life. . . . History, tradition, culture are all very well in their way; but they are not enough . . . to throw off the shams and trivialities that cramp and stifle life—that is what we need. And another way of putting it is this: I want a vision of Man. I want to perfect my vision of the archetypal forms of the human spirit. I want to see Man and Woman and Childhood and Adolescence and Old Age, as Blake saw them; and still more I want to discern the forms of Joy, Courage, Mercy, Love, Innocence, and Wisdom, as in their essence they are." He paused and then added in another tone: "But I expect you find this sounds rather woolly."

On the other physical plane is the intimacy with Stephen which, of course, exists in time and which is thus subject to its frustrating power, as the moment for his departure draws near. Paulina states the dichotomy:

"We are puppets, piteous puppets. Tom must die. Stephen must go away. I must stay. And something tells me I shall never see Stephen again. All this, measured in terms of happiness, is terrible; but there is another measure of things, I suppose—or perhaps another happiness? I must try to find it, and Tom will help me. I feel that in imagination he is able to share in the life of the earth as a whole. I sometimes feel him to be inhabiting not only his little house but all the great cities of America, aware of the desperation that is gripping the people like a black frost—and he is also upon the empty oceans, on the dusty Asian plains, and in the jungles of the Tropic South. I feel him to be aware of the hungry toiling populations of India, China, and Russia."

Just before Stephen leaves, the three visit the grove—the religious counterpart to the scene of physical passion between Stephen and Paulina. In the midst of the trees, despite her desire for comfort and her resistance to the place, Paulina senses the Ancient of Days. Wentworth is lost in his cosmic musings: in the endeavour to understand the spiritual forces of the world lies the greatness of Man. Yet all is not *merely* dark. Here the three are together in a sort of mystical, super-sexual union; and here Paulina makes her final decision to wait with Tom.

Stephen leaves her, and she returns to the peace of the forest with which she is now familiar. Here, until the death of Tom, she achieves a certain inner harmony. She is soon seized up in the remoteness of the setting; and gradually settles into a contentment with her identification with nature—into a "secret pool of beatitude beneath the crust of the external world." For a time she is "suspended in a region outside the real world." A more and more vivid sense of the spiritual takes hold of her, despite her remembrance of the rest of the world and of its *unawareness* of spiritual truth.

Tom dies after his final vision of man—through the eyes of God—the Man who yet "*struggles hard.*"

Consider the standards that he sets himself—his ideals of courage, of gener-osity, of endurance! Consider not only Man's disinterested devotion to truth, but his passion for nobility, his restless search after greatness. Consider that un-conquerable fastidiousness which forces him to toil in order to bring the poor, flesh-bound, witless creature that he is a little nearer to what he wishes to be.

Paulina feels now that she must go to Russia—to the new life which exists between the old social order and the ultimate Vision. She cannot be a cause of Stephen's giving up Russia—despite its materialism, as Tom says, "a new civilisation, a better life, are being attempted there . . . Regeneration is there." Then a telegram arrives telling of Stephen's death. The hope lies with Matthew the child: she goes to him. For in her desolation is the thought "Matthew is still alive".

The problems of contemplation and action, then, are explored through the persons of Wentworth and Stephen respectively: they represent, of course, different sides of Myers's nature. "The book *is* based (to a certain extent) on an episode in his own life—but he, of course, is neither Stephen nor Wentworth—something of both." In-deed, one feels the book, despite the exotic setting, to contain an auto-biographical element; and that Paulina's staying with Wentworth rep-resented a certain wish-fulfilment. The book is perhaps stronger in its exposition of the contemplative side than in its search for the new civil-isation, for the cosmic sense of humanity revealed by Wentworth is too diffuse in its expression to yield much positive impetus to action. Again, both men die, though their deaths may have been a way out of a diffi-culty. Myers had much trouble with the ending.

L. H. Myers to Mrs Frances Partridge, 1 December, 1935:

In another registered envelope I am sending to you my naive and sentimental little tale. I should like you to run through it the first time as a story, *without thinking of proof-reading*, for I should like to know how it strikes you, and you need not be afraid of hurting my feelings by telling me. The last two chapters are in type, for I have been baffled by them. I'm afraid at this point I began to lose interest in my characters; and that is the weakness of the tale that the climax comes before one can write Finis. In fact the whole of Part III requires a *tour de force*—and I cannot flatter myself that I have risen to the occasion, although there are parts that I like very much.

One cannot help sensing the strength of the desire to retreat, and one is not surprised to read, later in the same letter: "I am feeling very ill, and *Paulina* is my swan song or goose croak." (*Paulina* was the name first given to the book.) Of the two possible responses to the evils of the social setting, that of the Yogi or of the commissar, of retreat or ac-tion, it is only the first that is examined with any thoroughness; and the praise of the new social order in Russia is fitful and grudging. The mystical element predominates, so that even love becomes a retreat into nothingness—even 'death'—rather than an active state; through it Myers seems to achieve rest from strife rather than an impetus to further action.

Yet, in the final analysis, the claims of 'life' are met. The "little tale" is not too sentimental because the presence of pain is a constant reminder of the claims of life. The study is not a complex one; it translates the terms of its problem into comparatively naive symbols. The final effect of the book is perhaps of a certain incompleteness; for the positive impact of the values of the forest on Paulina is never allowed time to reveal itself; nevertheless, the gesture is made; she is to rejoin Matthew. Moreover, Wentworth's mysticism involves an appreciation of humanity; it is not a retreat into the realms of pure being. The ideal of 'self-illumination' is not, he considers, incompatible with the 'ideal of social duty'. Wentworth makes no very vital impact; though through his influence on Paulina and Stephen he can yet work on the world of social relationships. Paulina's retreat, in fact, is analogous to that withdrawal of which the Guru speaks to Jali.

What is being sought is a stability, in terms of which the dynamic elements of life will have significance, a centre from which the human mind can start out on its quest, an assured basis from which action can derive its significance. The title, *Strange Glory*, is taken from Traherne's poem:

> A Stranger here
> Strange things doth meet, strange Glory see;
> Strange Treasures lodg'd in this fair world appear,
> Strange all and new to me:
> But that they mine should be who Nothing was,
> That strangest is of all; yet brought to pass.

Paulina starts as nothing—a 'ghost'. The 'treasures' she gathers during the course of the book are intended to provide her with the spiritual capital for her journey; the two men, Wentworth and Stephen, have both taken a hand in her development, have both added the peculiar essence of what in life they have stood for to her being; and at the end she accepts the new life which Matthew, Stephen's child, offers her.

A certain dissatisfaction with the novel springs, perhaps, from the fact that its symbols are not translated into sufficiently concrete terms, that there is a certain paucity of 'felt life'. A relevant comparison is with *St Mawr*, Lawrence's *nouvelle* which offers a more firmly grasped handling of a somewhat similar theme. Myers can only offer his criticism of contemporary life from the stand-point of retreat; thus, the

apparatus—it tends to be that too much—of swamp and forest is necessary to provide him with symbols in terms of which his criticism of
contemporary life can take significance; and those symbols, besides
being more commonplace and 'usual', lack the defined presence that
gives point to Lawrence's use of the horse. The difference emerges
partly as a difference of style; for, as Dr Leavis has pointed out, in
Scrutiny (Spring, 1950):

Lawrence writes out of the full living language with a flexibility and a
creative freedom for which I can think of no parallel in modern times. His
writing seems to have the careless ease of extraordinarily fluent and racy speech;
but you see, if you stop to cast a critical eye back over the page, that everything
is precisely and easily *right*—the slangy colloquialism, the flippant cliché given
an emotional intensity, the 'placing' sardonic touch, and, when it comes (as it so
marvellously can at any moment), the free play of poetic imagery and imaginative evocation, sensuous and focally suggestive.

Myers has none of these virtues; and this partly because he is not in such
superb command of his theme as is Lawrence; hence the feeling that
Strange Glory borders on the sentimental, that it contains more than a
hint of indulgence. Paulina's acceptance of the life of the forest is arrived
at a little too easily—at least in the terms of the novel. There is none of
that prolonged strife towards comprehension which makes Lou's rejection of Rico and her journey to Texas and the mountains of representative significance; and this weakness pervades Myers's appreciation
of the two men, Stephen and Wentworth. They are insufficiently *there*,
insufficiently individual in speech and outlook to give firmness and
point to the curious *ménage à trois*—for that is what it amounts to; the
cross-tensions of personalities are omitted. The reason is perhaps because
passion, to Myers, does not mean life and vitality, but a form of death
and forgetfulness. There is an insufficient carry-over between the 'ordinary' events of every-day life and the life of relationship, which has come
to be something dreamt of, apart from the stresses and strains of 'real'
life. The sexual life and 'ordinary' existence do not coalesce. 'Love' thus
becomes a 'relief' rather than an assertion of vitality. It is as if Myers's
mind is split and he is unable to bring together the two. (This aspect has
already been noted in *The Pool of Vishnu*.) Hence the hint of defeatism
—the tendency to exploit the theme of unsatisfactory social life and
timeless nature. For the 'social' implications of the Paulina-Stephen-
Wentworth relationships are never really hinted at—they are depicted
too much in terms of beautiful friendships. And so the positives which
the book has to offer lack force and vitality. There is no triumphant
re-assertion of 'civilisation' such as that which marks the conclusion of
St Mawr. The tale is not wholly unpleasing; it is written with enough

taste to prevent its becoming sickly or cloying. But it illustrates, perhaps better than any of Myers's books, the essential restrictions of 'fastidiousness', and the difficulties of giving body and substance to— making valid within the context of a novel—his transcendental yearnings. The pseudo-Jungian mysticism represents a gesture towards, rather than a firmly grasped achievement of, a religious consciousness.

CHAPTER VI

MYERS'S COMMENTS ON HIS
OWN WRITINGS

M YERS'S letters contain a few comments of interest on his own
work and on his methods of writing. Reference has already
been made to his slowness of composition, and to the fact
that he was over forty before his first work of importance appeared. "I
was always a very slow and fitful worker," he wrote to Mr Gai Eaton,
a young friend who had asked his advice, "and it took me ten years to
get out my first book after many re-writings." It was his custom to
write and rewrite—in this he was quite astonishingly painstaking,
Flaubertian: ". . . I always work up from the most pitiable stuff by
slow stages to what I really mean," and, à propos his attempt at a
sociological work at the end of his life, he informed Mr Huntington
that "the first version of anything I write is extremely inferior to the
final version. When I read over what I have just submitted to you I shall
be disgusted with it in many ways. But I think I shall find revision as
easy as I find the first draft."

The first ideas he would write down very quickly, scribbling rapidly
away:

Marchesa Iris Origo to the author:

Leo Myers took endless pains over his work. Each chapter was re-written,
revised, almost invariably condensed—before he was satisfied with it, and often
the whole sequence of events, the architectural structure of the book, would be
altered. But the *first flow* of inspiration would come very quickly; for several
days he would be absorbed by a compelling idea that had taken charge of him,
by some scene that compelled itself to be written.

He never learnt to handle the mechanics of writing with ease; semi-
jokingly he would refer to himself as "illiterate." He would ask advice
on how to get a character out of the room, or how to introduce him to
the reader. Sometimes the device creaked badly, as in the case of the
introduction of Smith the humanist in *The Root and the Flower*. He
would even seek guidance on humbler matters—on spelling, punctua-
tion, and grammar. Thus he asks Mr L. P. Hartley, 28 January, 1929:
"Does one say 'as if it *were*' or 'as if it *was*'? And 'He is cleverer than *I*'
or 'than *me*'. I wish I were/was not so illiterate."

When he had finished a draft, he would send it round to friends for their criticism (despite his statement in the following letter that it was against his principles to do so); and he was always anxious for advice.

L. H. Myers to Mr L. P. Hartley, 1929:

I am going to send off the first twenty-one chapters of my book to you. There are another eight to come. . . . It is against my principles to send unpublished books to friends like this, and to send a novel to you is a particularly reprehensible thing to do. I consider, however, that you may be able to give me some criticism of value, and I think sufficiently well of the book to feel that I must make it as good as possible at all costs. In other words I trespass upon your amiability deliberately. You will not of course hesitate to criticize, and I shall value all adverse criticism especially.

and in the next letter:

L. H. Myers to Mr L. P. Hartley, 1929:

I am sending you . . . the concluding eight chapters of Vol. I. I have read none of this (or the last batch) over. It is probably full of misprints and many chapters require (I am only too miserably aware of this!) a good deal of revision. There are nasty little patches.

I expect that if I put the whole thing away for a few months, on getting it out I should see at a glance that a great deal is rather pedestrian and could be conveyed to the reader by *implication* and *inference.* Can you pick out these patches for me? Can you tell me where the story drags and gets dull?

When advice was given, he often took it eagerly:

L. H. Myers to Mr L. P. Hartley, 1929:

Many thanks for your letter; I wish you could have pointed out many more defects and flaws—although of course it is too late to alter anything except flaws. I agree about Jali's conversation: I agree with all you say . . . I have read it over now and found something to alter on every other page. In fact the book is going to be rather carelessly turned out, I fear. The end chapters especially are just thrown together anyhow. But I am so bored with it all now. . . .

He was never really satisfied with his work. A time was reached, however, when despite himself it would bore him, and he would rush gladly to the end:

L. H. Myers to Mrs Mary Macdowall, 15 *July,* 1929:

I hope Arthur [Macdowall] is getting on with his book. I *scamped* mine at the end. I got so sick of it. And the thought of a second volume of it fills me with dismay.

But such self-accusations were perhaps not quite honest; for although he was in many ways very modest about his powers as a writer, he put much of himself into his books ("I am no good at letter writing . . . What I have I have put into my books") and was, moreover, strongly bound up with the ideas he expressed in them:

Marchesa Iris Origo to the author:

In his attitude to his work there was . . . a curious mixture of confidence and humility. On the one hand he *knew*, deeply, that his work was good, and important. On the other—where details of structure, style, characterisation, etc., were concerned—he would ask for advice and criticism from others, and consider any suggestion with a most remarkable patience and even eagerness.

Even the expression of his boredom did not prevent careful last minute scrutinies and an extraordinary care over detail. It might lead to a certain frenzy: "I am so distracted by everything, —especially by my book which I am trying to finish by the end of this month"; or his work would help during a difficult period:

L. H. Myers to Marchesa Iris Origo, 1939:

During these months I have worked harder than ever before in my life. It has been very slow, toilsome, uphill work. (I made about six false starts at the Jali and Guru at pool chapter.) And there is nothing like work to produce serenity.

or a lassitude would descend: "I have told Cape that I will provide Vol. II [i.e. of *The Root and the Flower*] in six months' time. It will certainly be eighteen months' time. I can tell you I am pretty fed up." He recognised that such lassitude was part of the creative process, however. "Remember," he tells Mr Walter Allen (31 October, 1940) "that periods of mental emptiness or laziness are part of the process of writing a book." But when these periods descended, he was not too pleased: "As for me I have done no writing for months, and am wretchedly self-dissatisfied in consequence." Such contrariness, of course, is the lot of many writers: Myers's peculiar susceptibility to ennui tended to make the swing from avid interest to boredom particularly violent.

He never aimed at popularity, nor did he make any alterations in his books in order to appeal to a wider public. In the last resort he wrote always to please himself:

L. H. Myers to Mr L. P. Hartley, 7 July, 1929:

I am well aware that in this book I am giving people what *I* like—and with the inevitable implication: If *you* don't like it,—well, I'm sorry for you—But that is not the way to be popular.

He realised that there was no money to be made out of writing: "Frankly the project of making money by turning out good books seems to me utopian."

He was primarily interested in his novels as media for the setting out of certain ideas:

Marchesa Iris Origo to the author:

He regarded his novels merely as a vehicle for his *ideas*—and was *not* interested in the novel-form in itself—or even in *most* of his characters, except as a peg to the ideas they represented.

Many of these ideas were not such as to make him popular in fashionable literary circles—and he knew it. If he took pains never to write down to his public, and cared little for popularity, he yet of course wished to be understood and was thankful for praise:

L. H. Myers to Mr L. P. Hartley, 2 November, 1929:

The *Saturday Review* has just arrived and your review naturally has given me the very greatest pleasure. You have *done me fine* indeed!—and of course with a discrimination that shows that you saw exactly what the author meant to do.

When the reviews were unfavourable, or likely to be so, he had sufficient detachment not to be unduly upset; thus he writes about *The Pool:*

L. H. Myers to Marchesa Iris Origo, 1940:

I hope so much that you won't be disappointed with the reception which this book gets. . . . At any rate, you mustn't feel disappointed on *my* account. I am strong in my own conceit. I like and admire my book, and see clearly that that is a good reason for expecting others not to like or admire it. For when I consider what books that have come out recently are liked by others I find that they are not books that I like, and *vice versa. The Clue to History, Poetry and Anarchism,* for instance, have had (especially the first) bad reviews and a poor public . . . I feel that this is a grown-up book, and very few people are grown-up. Also this book is a censure. Many people will obscurely feel themselves censured.

He realises then, that his object was one that not only would be displeasing to many people, but one that would actively antagonise a number. And what that object was, at least in *The Root and the Flower,* he explains:

L. H. Myers to Mr L. P. Hartley, 2 November, 1929:

It *was* my object to create a world that I liked better than the existing one,—a rather presumptuous object because it is really too much to expect other people to swallow down one's own particular predilections *en masse.* But this, as a form of criticism is superior to my mind, to the everlasting sneering and objurgating of such as Aldous Huxley. In all those people too, I think I detect a secret admiration for a great deal of what they denounce. My method is at any rate a method of *constructive* criticism.

The need to be constructive enabled him to preserve a careful balance even at a time when the expression of his opinions in private was becoming increasingly violent. It prevented his relying on any cheapness of effect by which he might win some applause, but which would weaken the impact of what he wanted to say. Thus he writes to the Marchesa Iris Origo, 1939. "I shall take out certain bits about Lakhi [i.e. Lakshmi], which I think rather cheap. Any tincture of spite weakens the effect." But that did not lead him to mitigate his effects. He realised the danger of a lukewarmness which, in the name of fair-mindedness, prevented all vigour of effect and which would in any case be out of place in a novel. Thus he did believe that his "basic condemnation of Lakhi should not be qualified—I do feel Lakhi to be a definite person, and a person to be condemned (in so far as any human being is ever to be condemned)." (Letter to the Marchesa Iris Origo, 1940.) His attitude can be seen in the way in which he answers Stapledon's criticism of his handling of Smith the humanist in *The Root and the Flower*:

L. H. Myers to Olaf Stapledon, 14 September, 1934:

Let me admit at once that I feel that Smith does *not* represent humanism at its best. But in a novel unfairness of this kind is, I hope, excusable,—Smith standing not so much for the doctrine as for a type professing the doctrine. Well can I understand that with the memory of a very different kind of individual in your mind, the doctrine has been seen by you at its best—and, indeed, I have no doubt I should feel about that individual, and about the doctrine *as held by him*, all the sympathy that you feel. But I have not wanted to make Smith intellectually inadequate; I have tried to make him talk with sense and vigour; and I should be deeply grateful to you if you could give me a hint of what more to put into his mouth. If you can think of any place where he might have got in a good blow, and didn't,—I wish you would tell me. Similarly, if the Rajah has said anything *very* stupid, do tell me.

That you can really feel inclined to read the whole book I can hardly believe. You must be very busy, and I do not like to bother you with it. Actually, I show up the Rajah later on—I mean I disassociate myself from him—but not of course in favour of Smith. . . .

I am going to alter some sentences spoken by Smith because they are practically 'lifted' unchanged from *The Greek View of Life*, and that is not very good taste. I don't want to caricature G. L. D.

and in a second letter:

L. H. Myers to Olaf Stapledon, 19 October, 1934:

I have been reading over *The Near and the Far* and *Prince Jali* in order to revise them: and I found them very *un*interesting. With regard to your criticisms, I agree with you that I am prejudiced against humanism, and I fear that my vindictiveness may be a weakness in the book. I have already considered putting a humanist of a better type in somewhere; I shall, if I can. But I shall find it hard to find a man without the defects of most kinds of humanists. I should not call *you* a humanist.

He took much the same line where Stapledon's criticisms of his anti-aestheticism were concerned; he realised the faults inherent in his undertaking and the danger lest, as an experiment in philosophical fiction, it should end up by being neither philosophy nor fiction:

L. H. Myers to Olaf Stapledon, 19 October, 1934:

Again, I agree with what you say about the present day situation of aestheticism. Your analysis seems to me extraordinarily true and good. In a very few words you express the gist of the whole matter. But here we must distinguish between an essay on aestheticism and a novel in which aspects of aestheticism are exhibited. I am afraid the novel form forces one rather into unfairnesses. Anyhow I do not see how to reconcile the requirements of drama—I mean action, strong light, and shadows, etc.—with a balanced exposition of rights and wrongs—still less with an *explanatory* attitude. (You, on the other hand, in L[ast] and F[irst] Men did manage,—indeed one of the greatest merits of the book is the extraordinary fairness and balance of judgment shown. But your fictional framework was cleverly contrived *ad hoc*.) I am rather afraid I have not at all avoided exposing myself to criticism from two different stand-points, that of the novel-reader and that of the philosopher. The fictional items: Amar's fever, the death of Amar's servant, Dantawat, etc. belong more to the story *as a story* than to the story as a treatise. Nevertheless all these items do bear upon the psychological condition of Amar, and do indirectly have a philosophical significance—or at any rate they are intended to. The most one can hope to do in a book of this kind is to be "suggestive";—a compromise between philosophy and fiction, it was foredoomed from the start to great defects.

He appreciated the need to be explicit, the necessity of making clear to his readers just what he was getting at—the fundamental drift of his argument, what in fact he had to offer *positively*:

L. H. Myers to Olaf Stapledon, 31 July, 1936:

I am now getting on with the second half of *The R[oot] and the F[lower]*—and I have in mind, as I do so, your observation that not yet do I give the reader a sense of getting my meaning—which should also be a real sense of alimentation —although of course an *explanation* of the mysteries of the cosmos can hardly be expected of [me].

As we have seen in his reply to the criticisms offered concerning *The Pool of Vishnu*, he understood that he must write of what interested him. His books were intended to have a significance for the contemporary world—and to assert a possibility of human nature that few contemporary writers had appreciated:

L. H. Myers to Mr Gai Eaton, 21 May, 1943:

As for *The Near and the Far*—yes, I suppose the end-part (Vishnu) breathes serenity—but that was not my intention. My intention was to portray a good man. (There are many in the world all the time, but only knaves and fools are portrayed as a rule.) And a good man exhales an atmosphere of serenity. Actually, the Guru does not preach a doctrine of serenity, however. Nor do *any* of the other characters find a resolution of their difficulties and conflicts. I think your suggestion that I put serenity into the book instead of finding it in my own life, is shrewd and, in fact, right.

Yet this assertion of "goodness," this probing of aspects of the human mind so much neglected by his contemporaries, was not something he regarded as unusual until it was pointed out to him:

L. H. Myers to Mr Walter Allen, 7 June, 1940:

I did of course intend the book to have contemporary relevance. (My only fear was that in this volume I was overdoing it—doing obvious propaganda and preaching *at* the reader.) But I was not consciously aiming at anything unusual in the way of characterisation. Now that you point it out to me, however, I do see that you have put your finger on an important difference between my view of human beings and the view of the authors you mention. I think the other view was, historically, called for—and will always be useful as a corrective to the romanticism (if it is that) of my view. But I like to think—and I am very glad *you* think—that my view is not untruthful, and that it does assert a dignity in the human mind that is truly there. This is a subject that I should much like to discuss with you.

There was in Myers, that is to say, no conscious straining after effect; the 'dignity' of the human mind was something implicitly felt rather than consciously worked up as a novelistic device.

Sometimes he would look back over the books he had written. His comments on them would be frank and often very unfavourable:

L. H. Myers to Mr Walter Allen, 16 October, 1940:

I have found a copy of *The Orissers* which apparently is Isherwood's. I don't know him, and how it came into my possession I can't imagine. Opening it at random I find it *quite* intolerable. I blush. But perhaps if one goes at it from the beginning, one finds some quality which carries one along. For God's sake, don't try to read it until you have unlimited leisure; and even then better not try at all. I'm trying to get hold of a copy of *The 'Clio'* which I believe to be, at least, slick.

Though for a long time *The 'Clio'* was not a novel that he thought much of, towards the end of his life he saw virtues in it that he had perhaps taken too lightly before.

L. H. Myers to Mr Gai Eaton, 1943:

Unable to find light literature I am reduced to reading The '*Clio*', and am surprised by its qualities. It is depressing to think that if I have gained something since, I have also lost a lot.

When his books appeared, they were frequently praised by contemporary reviewers for the sensuous beauty of their settings and the excellent descriptions of natural scenery that they contained. That Myers never visited any of the places that his books described—the nearest he got to India was Ceylon—has already been mentioned. The Amazon, India, and the Louisiana swamps were all places that existed for him entirely in his own mind.

Myers was never a lover of nature—a matter of some regret to him because of his inability to gain sustenance from a contact which many spiritually sensitive men had been able to enjoy. "I'm afraid I do lack in certain responses to nature," he wrote, though there is a letter in which he speaks of the "solace" of "gardens and gardening." Of his later years, George Orwell writes:

He also cared nothing for possessions. He had a beautiful garden and a good many acres of land surrounding his house, but he was frankly bored with it when he showed me round it. He said he could not be bothered to cultivate the land or keep animals on it—it was a kind of rough pasture—because he had no interest in that kind of thing.

On one occasion, when out walking with a friend, he was drawing a contrast between her ability to gain spiritual sustenance from a walk in the country, and his own entire indifference: "Look at the primroses," he finished up in a mood of exasperation, "the bloodiest flowers there are." Thus, the presence in his novels of much description of nature was to him a matter of indifference. When he was praised for this aspect of his work he would wave all compliments aside, saying that to him such descriptions were of no importance. He was interested only in the human conflict and the ideas which lay behind it.

CHAPTER VII

BIOGRAPHICAL SKETCH

THE essential things, when considering Myers as a novelist, are some account of the circles within which he moved and the nature of his views and interests. The Myers are a distinguished family; now that he has been enshrined in the *Dictionary of National Biography*, Leo Myers will represent the fourth generation of his family in the direct line of descent to be so honoured. His paternal great grand-father, Thomas Myers, Ll.D., was, in 1806, appointed Professor of Mathematics at the Royal Military Academy, Woolwich, and published works on Geography, Mathematics, and Education. Frederic, Thomas's son, after an outstanding career at Clare Hall, became perpetual curate of St John's, Keswick in 1838 and enjoyed the friendship of distinguished contemporaries such as Jowett, Arthur Stanley, and the Wordsworths until his death in 1851. His chief work was *Catholic Thoughts*, an attack on the High Church movement; in it he deprecated the inequality of spiritual privilege implied by the emphasis on a theoretic creed and the presence of a priestly caste. The liberal protestant note, characteristic, in varying degrees, of his descendants, was firmly struck; the book was only published posthumously in 1874, for fear of its disturbing the faith of others. His son, Frederic W. H., born in 1843, was Leo Myers's father.

F. W. H. Myers has a minor, though not undistinguished, place in Victorian letters. He made Leckhampton House, where Leo was born in 1881, one of the centres of Cambridge intellectual life. An indifferent poet (his *St Paul* created some stir, though it seems turgid to-day) he published a number of literary essays which were respected, though they are not comparable with those of, say, Leslie Stephen in keenness of penetration. He knew many of the literary figures of the day, George Eliot, Tennyson, etc. What he sought in literature, in a way oddly similar to that of his son, was a set of attitudes which coincided with a certain range of moral feelings; the poets he praises find favour as 'prophets'—his Wordsworth is the exponent on a religion of nature, his Tennyson "a sage . . . whose wisdom is kindled with emotion."

It is, however, as one of the founder members of the Society for Psychical Research that he made his chief mark on the intellectual history of his time. There he joined with his former tutor, Henry Sidgwick the first President of the Society, Edmund Gurney, Frank Podmore, Lord Rayleigh, Charles Richet, and others in the investigation of psychical phenomena. He dissociated himself from all dogmatic beliefs, urging their irrelevance in the present state of knowledge. Through his psychical researches he endeavoured, as he put it, to re-enter the heavenly mansion by the scullery window after having been kicked out of the front door. (The phrases are taken from his autobiography, *Fragments of an Inner life*.) His researches led to the publication of two large tomes, *Human Personality and Its Survival of Bodily Death*, a fascinating indication of the late Victorian attempt to bolster religious faith through scientific investigation. His main purpose was to prove the immortality of the soul; and he died convinced of his success. The book lacks rigour by modern scientific standards; but William James, who knew Myers well, found his concept of the subliminal consciousness "the most important step forward that has occurred in psychology since I have been a student of that science."[1]

Leo Myers's home, then, took intellectual pursuits for granted. It was a somewhat perturbing home for a highly-strung child; and the reaction of the young Leo and of his younger brother and sister to the presence of the various mediums (such as Euspasia Palladino) brought there for investigation was one of mingled amusement and terror; the apprehension of the young Jali at the opening of *The Root and the Flower* ("spiritual presences moved. He was surrounded. Gradually he felt his skin tighten . . .") seems to have been drawn from these personal experiences of his father's research work. Certainly, there is plenty of evidence that the child was present at a number of investigations.

The father expected of his eldest son a quickness of intellectual advancement that was not forthcoming; and the boy went in some fear of his father, whom in later life he described, a little unjustly, as "Theodore Pontifex the Second." For his mother, a woman of strong and highly emotional personality, who "adored him with a passionate, unwavering, spoiling possessiveness" he developed over the years an ambivalent attitude of strong affection combined with cool ironic mockery. Evelyn Tennant's background was as intellectually distinguished as her husband's; for they met at the salon of her mother in Richmond Terrace, famous as the meeting place of political, literary, and artistic celebrities. Her beauty attracted the attention of several distinguished Victorian painters; and she sat for Watts, Millais, and Hennell. At a time when photography was still very much at an experimental stage, she set up a studio in Leckhampton House; and Gladstone, Browning, Irving, Arthur Balfour, among others, sat for her.

It was at Eton that one of the characteristic features of Leo Myers's life first revealed itself. For there he reacted strongly against the local

---

[1] Cf. a fuller account of F. W. H. Myers's views: G. H. Bantock, *The Scullery Window* (*Cambridge Journal*, June, 1948).

atmosphere; the exaggerated hierarchical distinctions, the rules regulating minutiae of personal conduct, the subtle arrogance of the Etonian of the day which, in the words of one of Myers's friends and contemporaries, Mr Charles Meade, "would excuse murder," formed a microcosm of the "great world" he so strongly criticises in his novels; and even thus early he turned against it. Another of his Etonian contemporaries, Mr A. J. Hugh-Smith writes that "Leo . . . was in some mysterious way a bitter rebel. Eton could well have helped that." He was not personally unpopular; he coped quite adequately with some initial bullying, and after that had no difficulty in being accepted as much as he wished to be accepted. Though he despised the cult of athletics, he was himself conspicuously successful as an athlete. There seems little doubt, then, from the comments of his contemporaries, that his peculiar susceptibility to a particular social tone was already developing, and did as much as anything to define his reaction to the school. Intellectually, he developed little: "He got through his school work quickly and easily but not industriously." His tutor, Arthur Benson he disliked as "a bulwark of the existing system," a "heygate," in the terminology of the day. Myers later said that he spent much of his life exploring the various Illusions which the human scene afforded. His life is composed of a series of rejections of social groups to which he belonged—and Eton was the first. Yet some of the friendships he formed there, notably with Mr C. F. Meade, Sir Charles Tennyson and Mr A. J. Hugh-Smith, lasted for many years—in the case of the first until Myers's death.

Immediately after leaving Eton he went to Germany to learn the language; his father, despite his disappointment with Leo's intellectual attainments, was bent on his entering one of the higher grades of the civil service—possibly the diplomatic service. Characteristically, he disliked the strongly aristocratic tone of German society. But it was in Germany that Leo had a prolonged, easy, and happy affair with a working-class German girl. He had previously been seduced by a girl two years his senior in a Swiss hotel where he was spending a holiday with his family. These were the first of many such encounters "ranging from the very squalid to the romantic," as he expressed it in a letter to Mr Gai Eaton.

Returning to England, he spent a short time at Cambridge; but his time there was cut short by the death of his father in January 1901, and he was forced to take care of his distressed mother. They undertook a visit to America where Frederic Myers had arranged a posthumous meeting with his wife, a meeting which failed to materialise. There two events of outstanding significance took place.

The first was a mystical experience he had in a hotel bedroom in

Chicago. The experience in itself was not one of any great visionary impact; but, in later life, it appears to have constituted a proof that experiences beyond the purely rational existed and thus it took on something of the quality of a touchstone. A sense of contact with the Infinite stimulated his religious awareness, and provided a standard by which the fopperies of the world could be judged.

The second event was his meeting with Miss Elsie Palmer, daughter of General William Palmer, at Glen Eyrie, Colorado. Though Miss Palmer was nine years older than Myers, and he was still a very young man, he proposed. Miss Palmer would not hear of marriage, though she liked the boy; and Myers had to wait seven years before they were finally married. Two children, both girls, were born of the marriage.

One of his significant friendships at this time was with Anne Douglas Sedgwick, the novelist, whom he met at the house of Lady Stanley, his aunt. She describes him at this period in a letter as "melancholy, sceptical, detached, very fastidious and delicate and sensitive." Her influence on his development is conjectural; but certain phrases from her letters—about how "morally and mentally vulgar some very nice people are," and her emphatic assertion that "only things founded on *human* relations attract me" would seem to show some obvious points of contact. Like Myers, she felt the same "horrible acute scepticism about the basis of everything"; at least she appreciated his difficulties; and her affection for him made him into the hero, Gavan, of one of her novels, *A Shadow of Life*, a hero who, like Myers, "saw himself at Eton in the hedged-round world of buoyant youth, standing apart, preoccupied, indifferent." Gavan's attempted suicide is oddly prophetic.

Myers's literary interests were developing. He conceived an interest in Dostoievsky, and his first literary effort was an attempt to turn *The Idiot* into a play. His first published work was *Arvat*, a play which appeared in 1908, but which has deservedly disappeared from view. Written in blank verse, it expresses an adolescent *weltschmerz*, but it is interesting to note the theme of a corrupt society appearing:

> Incarnate evil fingering bloody gold,
> Small hopes, ambitions petty, vain desires
> . . . This is the life of Men,
> The corporate life, Society, which I
> Have made my God, slaying the God in me.

In other ways, he lived the life of an idle, rich young man. He visited Egypt, Italy, and other countries; he raced at Brooklands, and made an adventurous ascent in a balloon, idled at social gatherings and fashionable restaurants; for in 1906 his god-father died and left him, in Anne Sedgwick's words, "quite well off." And indeed, it would be false to

think that, at this period or later, Myers was incapable of enjoyment;
Anne Douglas Sedgwick's romantic picture of the melancholy Gavan
needs to be balanced by a remark made by Mr Meade: "Looking back
over so much of our youth together, the predominant memory is constant laughter." Only his contact with a group of Birmingham business
people and his reaction to their handling of a strike among the work-
people indicated, in his social life, something of his simmering distaste
for his class; he parted company for good with these industrialists.

Anne Douglas Sedgwick's marriage to Mr Basil de Selincourt, and
Myers's own marriage led to a widening circle of friends. He had known
Miss Ethel Sands and Nan Hudson, literary and artistic hostesses, since
his undergraduate days. Miss Palmer merely joined a circle which was
looked upon as being a "picked little group after our own hearts and
amalgamating so perfectly: you (Mrs James Pitman), Nan, Ethel, Leo,
and Basil." About 1909 or 1910 he began *The Orissers*.

The war of 1914 appears to have taken him completely by surprise.
He volunteered perfunctorily and was rejected on medical grounds—
there was a suspicion of tuberculosis. But he threw himself into the task
of helping Belgian refugees and later became a clerk in the trade depart-
ment of the Foreign Office. Again, he reacted against the social tone,
although he formed a friendship with a fellow clerk, Allan Walton,
which lasted many years.

During all this time, he continued his work on *The Orissers*, though
really persistent work effort on the novel did not come until after the
war. Mrs Myers recalls vividly the number of times he would re-write
scenes, bringing them to her to re-read and returning to alter if she
found them—as she frequently did—crude. The work finally appeared
in 1922, through the agency of Mr C. Huntington of Putnam's; it had
a considerable *succès d'estime*; and we find Arnold Bennett noting in his
Journal: "Yesterday, highbrow tea at Ethel's [Sands's]. Logan Pearsall
Smith and L. H. Myers (author of *The Orissers*) and young Marjorie
Maden and me the guests. Myers a thin, dark man, *silencieux, un peu
précieux*, but apparently of a benevolent mind. Certainly a high-brow."
Apparently "the tea was a great success."

With the success of *The Orissers* Myers's circle of acquaintances
greatly extended. He came to know such writers as Mr E. M. Forster
(who found him, I am told, "chilly"), the Woolfs, Desmond MacCarthy
Mr L. P. Hartley, Lord David Cecil, the Rothenstein family, the
Sitwells, and many others who have exerted a powerful influence on
twentieth-century art and letters. Certainly, his entry into the literary
worlds of Bloomsbury and Chelsea with their Mayfair affiliations was
assured. He attended the literary gatherings of Lady Ottoline Morell;
he was seen at Gordon Square. And his attitude to these artistic groups

is of much interest. It provides an insight and criticism of even greater importance than that of D. H. Lawrence, because for so long he was of the group, accepted by them as one of their own. His reactions have their place and importance in the history of twentieth-century literature.

'Bloomsbury' was—and is—a world with a fairly well-defined attitude; a certain corporate spirit, the outcome of a concensus of assumption, a feeling of common worth, is discernible. To lump all the denizens together without allowing for idiosyncrasies of temperament and occasional heresies would be unjust; but there is a certain flavour, a tone, which characterises the work of the Bloomsbury group. The fact of constantly meeting together—due partly to a similarity of interest and partly to an accident of environment—has led to an almost unconscious assumption of a common judgment on the function of art in a hostile environment, a common estimation of the worth of each other's opinion in the front against the Philistine. As Mr Harrod shows in his book on Maynard Keynes, Bloomsbury developed from 'The Society' at Cambridge; not all members of Bloomsbury had been members of the Society, but Bloomsbury was, undoubtedly, "strongly influenced by some who had been members." If the group grew up "naturally and spontaneously," it nevertheless became "almost a family or clan." Mr Harrod brings out the iconoclastic element in the Society, under the leadership of Lytton Strachey, the close intimacy of personal relationship which manifested itself in a private language; letters and talk between members abounded in esoteric jokes and allusions. Though mockery and raillery at each other's expense were allowed, the members were bound together by a sense of "colossal moral superiority; their protestation of complete liberty of expression and a scepticism of outlook formed a barrier against an outer world in the grip of superstition and convention." There was even a Bloomsbury Voice—"emphatic but restrained" —with its peculiar cadences and insolences of effect. Maynard Keynes, in his paper "My Early Beliefs" completes the picture. Under the influence of G. E. Moore's *Principia Ethica*, Keynes points out, "nothing mattered except states of mind," divorced from action, achievement, or consequences. "We recognised no moral obligation on us, no inner sanction, to conform or to obey . . . Social action as an end in itself . . . dropped out of [our] Ideal." Hence their aesthetic notions became divorced from the life of society, and personal relationships became an end in themselves; their humanism was that of a highly self-conscious coterie which had too little basis in anything but itself.

Even a perfunctory knowledge of Myers's own position would be sufficient to indicate the grounds for his reaction against the sense of superiority and self-regard enjoyed by the Bloomsbury group. His

belief in the transcendental clashed with their humanism; personal relationships, as he makes clear in *The Pool of Vishnu*, were to be extended
to the life of society at large, not to provide an end in themselves.
Ultimately his is the morality of social action, not that of private
aesthetic contemplation; and his particular fastidiousness reacted against
the self-enclosed superiority and confidence of worth which character-
ised the group. His peculiar susceptibility to social tones would in itself
have been sufficient to make the highly self-conscious Bloomsbury
manner repellent to him. Minds which all too loudly proclaim their
complete freedom from prejudice and convention, in the end come to
accept the most boring of all conventions—the convention of unconventionality; for the mind which asserts its own autonomy (what
civilised man needed, considered Mr Clive Bell, was "complete development and self-expression") succumbs to the deadliest of tyrannies—
that of itself.

Thus Myers's reaction against Bloomsbury was assured. To personal
distaste was joined intellectual and moral disagreement. The process of
disentanglement was admittedly a much longer one than in the case of
Lawrence. In both, the instincts of reverence, indeed of worship, were
there, though manifested in different ways; a philosophy which turned
"states of mind" into absolutes instead of assessing the moral value of
those states of mind would inevitably become repugnant to both.
Myers was at first flattered by the attentions of this literary group—he
went through a violently snobbish phase, and was angry with his
daughter for not marrying a peer; he even wrote *The 'Clio'* to prove
that he could cope with the light, fashionable novel. Between 1926
and 1932 he belonged to *The Cranium*, a dining club to which many of
the Bloomsbury and Chelsea intellectuals belonged. But he was writing,
in 1927, to Mr L. P. Hartley:

> The taint of the Woolf will have worn off a bit, I hope, by the time we get
> there . . . How tactless of —— to say "the best company in the world." *We*
> know she is not.

And a friend of Myers writes that "he certainly admired Virginia
Woolf, but felt a curious antagonism from early on. They used to spar
together when they met in quite an unbridled way." Although he kept
on terms superficially friendly at least, with some of the group until his
last years, he gave public utterance to his distaste for the Bloomsbury
ethos in his portrayal of the Pleasance of the Arts in *The Root and the
Flower*: "In the Pleasance of the Arts, he was getting at the intellectuals
of Chelsea and Bloomsbury . . . Their cliquishness was their chief
crime, I believe, their intellectual snobbishness, their exclusiveness, back-
scratching, and jealousy," writes a friend who knew Myers well in

those years and with whom he discussed the writing of the book. Certainly, in considering his indictment one must make allowances for the dramatic needs of a novel, as Myers himself makes clear in a letter quoted in the previous chapter. Nevertheless it was moral rather than aesthetic worth that attracted Myers; and it was precisely here that he found Bloomsbury wanting.

It is perhaps relevant at this point to raise the question of Myers's own standards as manifested in his attitude to contemporaries. His taste was eccentric. He never formed his judgment in accordance with the fashion of the moment. The evidence concerning his reading matter, his critical comments revealed in letters and in the remarks of his friends bear out the peculiarly "unliterary" quality of his likes and dislikes. He was entirely uninfluenced by coterie values. He perceived that much of modern writing depended on a display of personality, a display which, because it omitted to submit the raw material of egotistical revelation of self to the moral judgment, resulted all too often in a form of exhibitionism. Experience was of little significance; it was only what experience could lead one to deduce about the fundamental nature of existence that interested him. Hence he tended to divide 'ideas' from literary form and expression. "When I come across a *live* book," he wrote to Olaf Stapledon (28 May, 1941), "I am so surprised and pleased that I just don't think about its patches of weakness. By a *live* book I mean one that (i) expresses a burst of vision and enlightenment, in the author, and (ii) is the expression of a true enlightenment, i.e. the vision of a truth." "He read books (as he got to know people) for their stimulating power and the ideas they contained" . . . "I think that what he increasingly looked for in books was the moral attitude underlying them; sincerity, unsnobbishness, something of the revolutionary. If that was 'all right', he was prepared to put up with a certain amount of crudity or even woolliness of style," write friends. Thus we encounter the same phenomena in his criticism of literature that have been noted in relation to his own writing. His judgment involved the application from the *outside* of moral standards, ideas, already formed; at his worst he lacked the capacity to 'feel into' a writer's use of language (as he lacked a vitally fresh apprehension of words in his own writing) and thus to submit himself to what might have involved a modification of sensibility. Because his ideas were subtler than those held by many people of his time, this is less serious in his creative work (although, as I have pointed out, it perhaps limits his appeal) than in his private critical judgments. It enabled him to make a telling point against Proust; but it also led him to over-value the work of writers such as Olaf Stapledon, whose attempt to blend scientific and imaginative insight into the nature of the cosmos in *Star-Maker*, for instance, called forth his loudest praises, displayed in a series of letters he addressed to Stapledon during the writing of that novel. He also had the greatest respect for Stapledon's *First and Last Men*, which he read several times, and of which he distributed copies to many of his friends. "He had," writes Mr Walter Allen, "a great admiration for Henry Green's *Party Going*, mainly because I think he read it as an exposure of the idle rich . . . Graham Greene he disapproved of because he was a Catholic, which was alone enough to damn him in his eyes . . . Of contemporary writers he thought most highly of Simenon, whom he claimed as great as Maupassant. He admired George Orwell and Herbert Read . . . In all these cases he was guided, I feel sure, by extra-literary judgment. His taste in poetry, he told me, was Tennysonian[1] . . . He was, of course, impatient of art as such; he had a vision of the good life and was interested only in those works which seemed to confirm it." Other fashionable writers he disliked were Aldous Huxley: "I think he is a sad example of the best that *un*creative mental ability can do"—and the Sitwells: "I find I cannot read Osbert for scorn"; the newer poets— Auden and others—found little favour and *Horizon* he distrusted.

This account of his literary tastes is, of course, far from exhaustive— I have already noted his fondness for Dostoievski; but it indicates sufficiently the idiosyncratic character of his enthusiasms and provides interesting confirmatory evidence of the equivocal nature of his literary interests. His main reading, indeed, was neither aesthetic nor literary. The work he most appreciated was of a scientific or philosophical tendency. The fashionable interest in psycho-analysis he shared; and he read much of Freud, Jung, and Adler with avidity, together with Karen Horney's developments and criticisms of Freudian theory. Jung's views on archetypal patterns exercised an obvious influence on *Strange Glory*; and he liked especially Jung's introduction to *The Secret of the Golden Flower*. He read widely in Eastern philosophy and religion, as is obvious from *The Near and the Far*; and the influence of Martin Buber's *I and Thou* and of some of John Macmurry's books is acknowledged in the Introduction to *The Pool of Vishnu*. Other authors cropping up in his correspondence and whom he read with varying degrees of attention were Bertrand Russell (about whom I shall say more later), E. S. Russell, Lloyd Morgan, Jeans and Eddington, Haldane and Julian Huxley, Joad and Jurgen Kuczynski—most, in fact, of the well-known writers of the inter-war years who had a socio-philosophical outlook. From many of them, because of their dissatisfaction with the current trends of society, he would cull material to lend weight to his own growing bitterness

---

[1] It was actually more extensive than this would suggest: Blake, Vaughan, Traherne, Emily Brontë, Hopkins, Yeats he liked; again he confesses to reading "Shakespeare with benefit"; but he admitted his own deficiencies of judgment where poetry was concerned.

with his own social class. He knew both George Orwell and Max Plowman and much admired the former's repudiation of upper class society and the sincerity and genuineness of the latter. Orwell's books he read and distributed widely.

Myers, then, was not a scholar; he distrusted the academic philosophers and was contemptuous of universities. What he looked for was 'vision' of a certain moral kind; hard thinking that led only to 'academic' conclusions he rejected. The word 'academic' was indeed to him a term of abuse, and the antagonism inherent in the picture of Mr Wilkinson in *The 'Clio'* was not untypical of his approach to the academic world in general. He disliked what he thought to be the spiritual deadness of the humanism which many scholars professed, and which he satirised in Smith in *The Root and the Flower*. Professional sociologists like Professor Ginsberg earned his particular contempt, because he failed to appreciate that their task was analysis rather than exhortation; and Myers, especially later, was a man with a mission. Towards the end of his life, he tended to read only what reinforced his strong, neurotically fixed, social views; he looked even more for confirmation rather than for fresh insights, and his reading habits became increasingly erratic. Frequently his mind would fly off at a tangent long before he had finished the book, with the result that he never read through to the end. "His reading habits were peculiar," relates a friend, "his mind often went off on its own at a tangent, leaving the author. He would give one some book (philosophy perhaps) and say: 'You must read this—it is extremely good and important'. I remember once his doing this: the first two pages were heavily scored and commented on in the margin. I read on and made some criticisms of something a little further on. 'Oh really?' he said, 'I only read the first two pages'." It must not be assumed, of course, that this was an invariable practice! Myers's reading did play an important part in his literary achievement. One of his novels was historical in context; and though no effort was made to keep the ideas with which he dealt contemporary with the setting, a certain amount of preliminary reading was necessary so that the incidents, at least, should not be anachronistic. But, much more important, the settings of his novels were, as has been pointed out, peculiarly mental. In some ways no novelist drew more directly on the experience which certain social settings and social tones afforded him; but Myers tended to see his characters in terms of the mental and philosophical traits which their conduct betrayed, and the happenings of his novels were related to the fundamental principles of conduct, his intuitions of the almost unconscious assumptions by which the characters were motivated. To term them "labelled figures moving in an exotic landscape," as a reviewer has done, does less than justice to the consistency of Myers's penetration and his ability to suggest the 'life' that animates a specific philosophical standpoint. Nevertheless, in the setting out of the different religious and metaphysical points of view he drew on his reading to a great extent. It is this fact which excuses and necessitates this brief account of his reading interests.

Myers's correspondence bears further witness to his interest in philosophy. It is amply clear that he was only an amateur in these matters, but his criticisms of some of the popular philosophical writers of his day have some bearing on the views he expressed in his novels; and since he is a 'philosophical' novelist, it is useful to see some of the themes which preoccupied him in the novels re-appearing in more direct exposition in his letters. Thus there has survived a long interchange with Olaf Stapledon, during which he urged, in a sentence reminiscent of the introduction to *The Root and the Flower*, that "there are certainly as many degrees of refinement of ethical and philosophical intentions as of aesthetic; and as aestheticism is often refined down to triviality, so does philosophical sensibility run a similar risk." (Letter dated 8 November, 1932.) He rejected some of the popular philosophers (or, as in the case of Bertrand Russell, whose contributions to modern linguistic philosophy Myers failed to appreciate, their more popular philosophical expositions) because of what he considered to be their latent exhibitionism, their lack of fundamental seriousness. Thus he writes to Stapledon: "In the case of Russell . . . I feel that philosophy is for him primarily a *jeu d'espirit*. He thinks out tricks and dodges by which traditional philosophic stumbling blocks may be got round." He felt that Russell avoided the metaphysical problem in which he himself was most interested, and which involved the reconciliation of scientific and spiritual knowledge, and hence failed to apprehend the universe as an order or system:

L. H. Myers to Olaf Stapledon, 28 February, 1932 :

He [i.e. Russell] throws up his hand just at the point where the metaphysician proper feels that he has to begin. We apprehend the world under a partial aspect of order, unity, and continuity; this aspect is imperfect but inescapable by the human mind . . . The fact is that Russell wants to disintegrate and maintain in a state of disintegration the data of experience which can only be artificially separated and which it is the business of philosophy ultimately to re-unite.

Thus Russell is taken to task for the omission of all axiological considerations: "The study of the ultimate *nature, reality,* and *significance* of values is in fact excluded from his philosophy. To my mind this stultifies his philosophy."

In his further criticism of Russell, Myers indicates how much he believes that life history and personality affect philosophic systematisation.

Value, for instance, depends on the existence of persons. In a long letter to Stapledon (24 March, 1932) he confesses to being puzzled over Stapledon's views on the objectivity of matter. "Personally, I find myself believing in the objective existence of matter as an uncharacterised substrate, of which nothing more can be said than that it is a convenient postulate as a locus for potential experiencings . . . We want a God's-eye view of the Whole, and I can't help feeling that that view should be holistic rather than atomistic, qualitative rather than quantitative . . . I attach more and more importance to modes of sensibility as means of apprehending the world." Thus he seeks to explain Russell's views in terms of Russell's own life history. He connects him with the general climate of opinion that prevailed in the inter-war years—its shallow pessimism and cynicism. He then comments on the perpetuation in Russell of the "youthful passion" of rebelliousness—"it revolts against authority in general; and this I take to be the keynote of Russell's character." (His general analysis bears a striking resemblance to Lawrence's comment: "What ails Russell is in matters of life and emotion, the inexperience of youth.") Thus he finds in Russell's hatred of God "a foil for the rebellion and self-worship of Man."

Such a belief in the 'personal' element in philosophy coloured Myers's discussions in other directions. He had a considerable interchange with Stapledon on the latter's sense of "the Whole," during which he pointed out that such a concept denoted "an extremely complicated apprehension of things, built up, partly by intuition, partly by 'reasoning': but essentially a construction of your own 'psyche' and labelled 'the Whole' by you."

It is interesting thus to confirm from his letters a matter he emphasised in the novels. It will be remembered how Gokal, in persuading Amar not to retire, urges that spiritual values do not exist "apart from personalities." Such a 'personal' philosophy, too, is inherent in Amar's final reaction to Daniyal, symbolising his realisation that the policy cannot be abstracted from the person who holds it. Moreover, in the novels the characters see the world as inherently bound up with their own personalities. One remembers Jali's appreciation that "the true self seemed to be isolated by its own inalienable nature from other true selves." The nature of the search for 'reality' behind the 'illusions' tends to emphasise the self-enclosed world within which each person lives. Myers's subjectivist philosophy, revealed in these letters as a vital element in his thought, indicates by its persistence and emphasis, one of the reasons why, in the last resort, he is not really successful in suggesting relationship. For to see life so much in terms of personality is to increase immensely the difficulty involved in acknowledging other 'knowing subjects' and, as I have pointed out, Myers is better at dealing with problems of isolation than he is at suggesting the complexities of relationship.

There is, however, one exception to his subjectivist standpoint—his belief in the objectivity of moral values. This belief is closely linked with his religious views on which his letters also throw light. "I believe myself to have a very strong feeling of the numinous," he stated on one occasion. Despite the mystical experience in Chicago, he was for long an agnostic, though he was "much against atheists and insisted on the possibility, which must be included in the agnostic's view, that religious dogma may be true," it has been explained to me. He was always intensely interested in science; but he condemned those who lived by science alone. And, as he grew older, the attractions of religion grew stronger. He came to feel that mystical experience was a form of contact with reality and the significance of his American experience grew stronger with age. He never arrived at any dogmatic beliefs; the Divine Being remained a mystery, not the centre of a carefully constructed cosmological system—in this he perpetuated the tradition of his family. But humanism was not enough; and the criticisms he offers of Smith's position in *The Root and the Flower* are frequently paralleled in his letters. Thus he writes to Olaf Stapledon in 1934: ". . . humanists too often make sociality an end in itself. They say, or rather they think: 'A good society is that which aims at making spiritually awakened individuals, and spiritually awakened individuals are those who aim at making a good society'. This vicious circle of small definite aims excludes true spirituality which always *comes from without*, and is only recognised for what it is *after* it has come." In further criticisms of Bertrand Russell—this time of his *Scientific Outlook* and *The Conquest of Happiness*—we can trace much of the thought which lay behind the Indian books:

L. H. Myers to Olaf Stapledon, 1934:

I have only skimmed *The Conquest of Happiness*. I gathered that he says happiness is reached by leading the "good life," and he has defined the "good life" as that which is inspired by love and guided by wisdom.

The love that Russell talks about is, however, in my judgment, fictive. Such "love" of Man is but the shadow of a hatred of God. I would, indeed, go so far as to say that no man can truly love his fellow men except as fellow-creatures, particles of the Divine. Russell's love exists and is estimable only in theory. Its simulacrum, however, is common enough. I am afraid a great deal of the pacifism and altruism we read about is inspired by it. This pseudo-love has its uses at the present time, I admit. People such as Lowes Dickinson and Leonard Woolf do useful work, for it has been necessary to break up old theologies and prejudices, and these armchair lovers of mankind can at least help to do that. But, in the long run, some very bad work will be done, if such people succeed in confusing and enfeebling the higher intuitions of mankind. I am more apprehensive of the evils of Russell's religion of God-hatred than of the more naive confusion between material and spiritual welfare, which, in different forms, are perplexing Russia and America to-day. . . . Russell's doctrine threatens the more civilised world with a malady of the spirit which will spread cynicism, indifference, and trivial-mindedness.

Thus Myers's moral conception of the good life was firmly rooted in his belief in the transcendental.

A Christian, secure in a specific set of dogmas by means of which God could be 'known' to the believer, might well describe Myers as having the will to believe rather than as a believer. He felt himself perpetually dissatisfied with terrestrial things, yet he was unable to submit his mind to any traditional religious discipline. Hence it is difficult to make clear what his sense of the numinous amounted to, in so far as it amounted to anything more than the apprehensions of a mind religiously inclined, but incapable by temperament or through the pressures of a sceptical age of accepting any fixity of religious organisation. He was often impatient of definition— and to such a mind vagueness provided at once an opportunity and a relief.

Myers's religious hankerings, of course, are closely linked with that anti-rational bias which he notes in the Preface to *The Root and the Flower*. He certainly did not deprecate, however, all use of the reason as I have noted in discussing the novels. What he wanted was a type of rationalism which would include, and allow for, the intuitive aspect of the mind. Thus he writes to Stapledon (28 March, 1932): "Are we sure that the universe is to be better apprehended by the reason than by intuition? Probably a blend of the two will give the best results. In a sense there *must* be a blend. Reason should control the blending as much as possible. This is a matter for the reason to consider, I think . . . that one of the most important activities of the reason is to 'plan' itself, to realise its limitations, and to consider to what extent the universe is likely to be rational, as man understands rationality." On another occasion (7 April, 1932), he thought that "the *opposition* between reason and intuition is illusory," though he desired to define as clearly as possible "what the *distinction* between them is." He certainly remained suspicious of irrationalism: "I don't think," he writes to Stapledon, "I am less sceptical of irrationalism than you. I am only, perhaps, more sceptical of most forms of rationalism." (14 December, 1932.)

Most of these comments belong to the early 1930s. Myers's last years are marked by a growing sense of isolation. The social and political events of the later 1930s provided ample fuel to stoke the fires of his social hatred. I have noted how he turned against nearly all the groups to which at one time or another he belonged—to Eton, the Foreign Office, Bloomsbury, and others. His last years were marred by a personal and social bitterness so intense that it led him to break with many of his oldest friends. He also made an attempt, which failed, to analyse for a wider public his loathing of the social order of his time. As late as 1932 he was politically conservative, though of course socially critical; and he always retained a sense of spiritual aristocracy in strong contradistinction to a social one. But the progress of events and his hyperfastidiousness in social relationships brought to the fore that strong mixture of hate and destructiveness which had always been part of his nature and which had led him, as a child, to ask: "Why is it that I always hate the things I hate more than I love the things that I love?"

This inability to attach himself to any community, however small, undoubtedly stimulated his emotional reaction against all organised groups. "T. E. Lawrence's neurosis drove him to become irretrievably part of an organisation: I have an opposite claustrophobic fear of organisations as such," he wrote to Mr C. Huntington. The only group he came to accept was one that he never saw—one that existed in his mind only as a dream of home. In actual life he was a strong individualist to the point of egotism; in fundamental aspiration he longed for some community to satisfy his social being. His sense of the importance, dignity and fundamental worth of human nature led him to find it inherently 'good'. Yet the circles in which he moved and which he analysed in his books were, in a number of respects at least, corrupt, ineffectual, and trivial. Blame, therefore, must be attached to a corrupt social order which *distorted* human beings and made them what he so often found them to be. His natural sensitivity associated, as such sensitivity often is, with irritability prevented his charity and pity from being released except intermittently. Instead, he projected his dream into a visionary state which he chose to call Russia. He was helped in his choice because Russia had, in fact, destroyed its ruling class and set up an order of society which he felt to be a significant improvement. He had, of course, never been to Russia, and he only knew about it from what he had read; but to criticise his emotional attraction to the country on these grounds is to attack on one plane what clearly existed for him very largely on another. Russia satisfied, in imagination, both the destructive and the constructive parts of his mind. For that reason, it provided the last illusion—the one which he was never able to outgrow. He was, moreover, convinced of the spiritual nature of the new society. In Russia spirit and enlightened social order seemed to meet, in a manner which did something to appease his religious aspirations.

Myers realised acutely, and from personal experience, how much class distinctions mattered in England. "Class cuts down to the bone. It can be transcended, but not annihilated, in personal relationships." He thought that power was so much in the hands of a small and restricted group that any hope of human betterment, any possibility of what he regarded as a juster social order, would need the liquidation of the upper class. His political allegiance was not unconnected with the view on personal relationships he expressed in *The Pool of Vishnu*. The whole tone and ethos of society, he considered, needed to be altered; and he half-thought this could be achieved at a personal level. "An alteration in the *tone* or ethos of society is what I think needs to be brought about," he wrote to Stapledon in 1940, "—which means a change of values. It is a thing that can be affected on a small scale and temporarily by a man walking into a room, if he is the right man." Again, to Mr C. F. Meade (1942): "*Persons* is what we all should be—not mere specimens of social types." Having broken with most of his old friends, Myers chose new ones who were for the most part of a left persuasion, like Plowman, Orwell, the Bernals, Mr Jurgen Kuczynski, and several Communist friends. He much admired the social idealism of Lilian Bowes Lyon, and another great friend who shared many of his views was the Marchesa Iris Origo. Politics, he thought, mattered—though, character-istically, he found something repellent about English Communists, whom he found "pretty bloody . . . especially the 'Parlour Commun-ists'—to which class I belong."

In order to further the cause he now so strongly had at heart, Myers attempted to do some writing. He tried three versions of a semi-sociological work, attempting to diagnose the evils of current society; he had in mind the publication of a Penguin Special. It all came to nought however—happily for his reputation. In the versions I have seen the familiar themes of the evils of the current class structure and the stultifying effect of tradition, which are much more convincingly analysed in *The Pool of Vishnu*, recur; the desire for a 'community of persons' rather than a society based on class, very much as expounded by the Guru, is expressed. But the form was uncongenial, and so he turned to an Autobiography, which could allow him to make the same points but in a more personal way. "My idea," he wrote to Mr Huntington, who took the keenest interest in the progress of these works, "is to use typical incidents, situations, and changes in my life to illustrate the sequence of my ideas." (26 December, 1941.) At first he seemed to be progressing well; the personal approach suited him better, and his circle of acquaintances had been extensive enough to afford him ample opportunity for the analysis of those whom he regarded as undesirable social types.

In the end all copies of what had been written were called in and destroyed. The opinions of those who read it varied. Some found it very amusing; most found it much more readable than the sociological ap-proach; but others felt that it was quite wrong—far too one-sided and unfair in its attack. On the whole, the political bias of the reader seems to have been a deciding factor in evaluation; thus a friend of strong left-wing views found in it a perfect exposure of the evils of the upper classes.

For the rest of his life, he became more and more wedded to his dream world of Russia. "Stalin's birthday: God bless him" appears at the head of a letter; and such comments as "our hearts are with Timo-schenko, and our attitude: who dies if Russia lives" recur. No accusa-tions of unfairness affected him: "Christ," he urged, "was not fair-minded." In part explanation of these outbursts, his growing ill-health and neurasthenia must be noted. Though he often displayed a strong sense of fun and was capable of the greatest good humour, he had all his life been a prey to depression of a neurotic kind. Towards the end of his life, letter after letter is concerned with his distaste for living, bears witness to his absorbed interest in anything connected with disease or expresses his profound *weltschmerz* and longing for release. He under-went frequent cures; and he developed a cancer phobia, so that even a gumboil necessitated an operation to disprove malignancy. As a young man he had tried to decide why men chose to live; no answer during his pursuit of what, significantly, he called the 'illusions' satis-fied him; and, latterly, he found living "a very over-rated pleasure." He was afflicted, too, by that guilt consciousness which attacked many of the more sensitive of his class at the time—one could instance George Orwell and Lilian Bowes Lyon among his friends. He was a Com-munist; but he immensely enjoyed good food and living—he was, in-deed, part owner of Boulestin's fashionable restaurant in London. His sense of isolation increased with the growing intransigency of his social and political ideas. For years he had threatened suicide; and on the night of 7 April, 1944, he took an overdose of vernal. He was found dead in his bed the next morning.

For all their frequent crudities, it would be highly unreasonable to dismiss Myers's social views—especially as subsumed in a much more refined form in the novels—as valueless. They reveal the reactions of a highly sensitive individual to a declining social order; and they further that indictment of certain sections of English upper class life to which Henry James, for instance, gave utterance. The "clumsy conventional expensive materialised vulgarised brutalised life of London," as the Master termed it, in Henry James's story, *The Lesson of the Master*, was one which both James and Myers condemned as evidencing unmis-takable signs of cultural decline. It is interesting, then, to recall that these two knew one another and that the number of their mutual acquaintances makes it clear that they moved in somewhat similar social circles—due allowance being made for the fact that Myers was much the younger man. When the full story of the Jamesian milieux is told, it, together with the further witness which, both then and at a later period, Myers can bear, will provide a fascinating chapter of our social history. Some aspects of those milieux, at least, will indicate the growing corruption of a vulgarised society without responsibilities and without moral sensibility.

It only remains to give a brief summing-up; for, in many respects, Myers possessed characteristics which, because his was a mentality of great delicacy, reflect the tensions, inhibitions, and conflicts of our era in a particularly discriminating way.

One thing that emerges about Myers—in contrast with, say, D. H. Lawrence, with whom in attitude he shows a certain amount of common ground—is his aloofness and detachment. Lawrence was isolated; but he always responded to the moment. Myers, with his exquisite manners and his carefully groomed appearance ("*un peu précieux*," perhaps, as Arnold Bennett saw him) lacked the vitality which drove Lawrence from the things he hated to seek new sources of life. Myers's integrity could not condone what was distasteful to him; but he was himself too much the product of the ethos he despised to dispense with it, as in their very different ways Orwell and Lawrence dispensed with theirs. He could only *detach* himself; he lacked the necessary force to attach himself to any new sources of life. And one cannot help seeing in this aloofness of his a certain egocentricity, even a betrayal of his own doctrines. Myers shows in his books how much he knows about social insincerities; his descriptions of their manifestations provide the chief excellence of his work. And the element of conscious control, of deliberate attitudinising which characterises so many of them, is indicative of the role they must have played in Myers's own life. For his novels are autobiographical in an intimate way. And yet the deep hatreds by which he was riven, especially at the end of his life, do not really appear. They seem to have come out in his life, in his hypochondria and his neurasthenia, his constant seeking for relationship and his equally constant failure to find it, rather than in his work. Myers, indeed, seems to have lacked that element of impersonality, that capacity to 'order' the emotions and intellect into a complex whole, which enables the great artist to project himself in an integral and ordered way into his fictional situations. It seems as if his mind and his emotions had suffered a division, as if there was no coherent centre from which he could emanate, as if the pressure of his personal life—his ennui, his need to find relief in furies of passionate hate against his class and the social order to which he belonged—were such that he had to leave a great deal out of his books which his artistic mind could not assimilate and transmute. Above all, there was his inability to bridge the gap between the passional-emotional and the intellectual and the way in which it has restricted the scope of his work.

Hence, one begins to see the significance of his comment to the effect that he tried to present in his last book a world that he liked better than the real one. Hence too, one realises why in writing *The Pool of Vishnu* he said "one can't write about what doesn't interest one, so it would be useless my trying to introduce sex or passion or romance more freely"; for sex was something, too, with which he could not come to terms. Clarified also is his lack of interest in nature, and the need which he had to provide a setting for his novels in places remote in time and place, as if he could not draw upon the concretely living present, as if he was insufficiently responsive to the life around him to gain sustenance from it. After all, Lawrence managed to provide at least as vital a presentation of contemporary problems in *Women in Love* as Myers does in *The Near and the Far*; and *Women in Love* is achieved by evoking the modern scene in all its immediacy.

Failure to get beyond himself meant that Myers's work was peculiarly mental; and it is not surprising to find that he was more interested in 'ideas' than in people, or that in his deepest relationships "there was a part of him that always remained detached, alone." Even the description from which the last sentence was taken speaks of his deep relationships as involving an "exactingness of truth" (exactingness towards himself, as well as to the other person) as if the thing was a matter of conscious effort. And, indeed, conscious effort must have played a very large part in this extraordinarily well-groomed existence. Yet "superficial relationships—with the railway porter, the waiter, the stranger next to him at dinner—he always found extraordinarily difficult and fatiguing." He had nothing of that capacity to give in immediate contact which, for instance, made the peasants love Lawrence so much, none of that vital apprehension of his immediate surroundings which invests Lawrence's description of ordinary people and things with a wonderful dignity and reverence.

And here we can see the relevance of another of Lawrence's comments; for there is a sense in which Lawrence's understanding of the modern world was of such a nature as to include within it an appreciation of the problem of such people as Myers himself. In the *Fantasia of the Unconscious* Lawrence points out:

Our leaders have not loved men: they have loved ideas, and have been willing to sacrifice passionate men on the altars of the blood-drinking, ever-ash-thirsty idea. Has President Wilson, or Karl Marx, or Bernard Shaw ever felt one hot blood-pulse of love for the working man, the half-conscious, deluded working man? Never. Each of these leaders has wanted to abstract him away from his own blood and being into some foul Methuselah or abstraction of a man.

For all his communism and his stated concern for the lower classes, Myers did not love men, certainly not in the way in which Lawrence did. I don't wish to suggest that Lawrence's relationships were, in the conventional sense, satisfactory. But one feels that his failures were due, partly at least, to his implacable unwillingness to accept those current insincerities of feeling and outlook without which relationship is so difficult in the modern world. Lawrence couldn't work his sympathies from what he calls "the upper centres"; he had to feel vital warmth and sympathy in his companion, and it is just this vital warmth and sympathy which the modern democratic community tends to inhibit.

Now, against this, Myers can only offer the 'ideal' of personal relationships. I call it the 'ideal' in Lawrence's sense of the term; for to leave the sex and the warmth out of his picture of Mohan and Damayanti is to leave out the basic springs of affection which bind men and women together; no account of a marriage relationship which leaves out these elements can be a full one, though it need not necessarily be negligible. There is an interesting passage in *Lady Chatterley's Lover* which serves as an explicit comment on *The Pool of Vishnu*:

"You see Hilda," said Connie after lunch, when they were nearing London, "you have never known either real tenderness or real sensuality: and if you do know them, and with the same person, it makes a great difference."

"For mercy's sake don't brag about your experiences!" said Hilda. "I've never met the man yet who was capable of intimacy with a woman, giving himself up to her. That was what I wanted. I'm not keen on their self-satisfied tenderness, and their sensuality. I'm not content to be any man's little petsy-wetsy, nor his *chair à plaisir* either. I wanted a complete intimacy, and I didn't get it. That's enough for me."

Connie pondered this. Complete intimacy! She supposed that meant revealing everything concerning yourself to the other person, and his revealing everything concerning himself. But that was a bore. And all that weary self-consciousness between a man and a woman! a disease!

"I think you're too conscious of yourself all the time, with everybody," she said to her sister.

"I hope at least I haven't a slave nature," said Hilda.

"But perhaps you have! Perhaps you are a slave to your own idea of yourself!"

As a criticism of Myers's idea of personal relationships this could hardly be more felicitous. For, indeed, Myers's idea is dependent on self-conscious assessment of the situation. Myers seems to have sought fulfilment through 'love' in that self-conscious sense of the term which Lawrence repudiates both in the social and the individual spheres. Lawrence, indeed, wanted community; but he wanted it in terms of deep sexual satisfaction and a unity in terms of fundamental purpose, something *beyond* the individual, instead of in terms of personalities. He

wanted people to meet on the "third ground, the holy ground"; he
was weary of that fingering over of their own souls, that sickening
"cloy of humanity" which the modern democratic world produced.
He realised his connectedness with the great processes of life: "I am part
of the sun as my eye is part of me." But to maintain this connection,
purpose and the strength of isolation must go into it—'isolation'—not
'detachment' in Myers's sense, which seems to me a different thing. For
'detachment' implies a conscious withdrawing from the situation, yet
a remaining emotionally involved to the extent of needing the situation as an emotional pivot, to exist, if necessary, in hatred of it.

What, I think, Myers needed was 'rootedness'—that is what all his
talk about 'community' amounts to. He was too conscious of living
in the "midst of all this disintegration" and of the difficulty therein of
thinking of "anything in the future." His sense of not belonging was,
of course, a source of strength as well as one of weakness. The weakness
comes out in his inability, fundamentally, to accept his position unequivocally. Isolation with him tends to become mere 'detachment'
which can be said to be neither one thing nor the other; for with the
stress that I am here intending it is too much involved, at the deeper
levels, with what it is seeking to be detached from. He was thus as an
artist unable to follow completely Conrad's injunction in the Preface
to *Under Western Eyes* to "strike and sustain the note of scrupulous
impartiality." Myers, for all his 'detachment', wanted an escape too
much from the ever-present burden of self through the acceptance of
some transcendental element; and he desired this as a means towards
integration in the wider life of community. Thus, for all his rejection of
the society of his time, he could not finally take his stand either in isolation or in relationship. He lived the rootless intellectualised life of to-
day; and despite his detestation of his class of society he was too involved in it to forgo its privileges, though he hated so much of its ethos.
Unlike his father, he could not even accept a harmony of common intellectual interests, a purpose in pursuit of a common truth; the bases of
his civilisation were too insecure. And even as an 'intellectual', he made
no connection with the common organs of the dissemination of opinion
of his day. He hated lecturing: he undertook no literary journalistic
work, he never broadcast. Only his books enabled him to make any
contact with the public of his times. Practically his only piece of occasional work was a Preface to Arthur Macdowell's *A Detached Observer*.

In addition to being a writer of great intrinsic interest, then, L. H.
Myers remains a peculiarly important—because highly sensitive—case-
history in the study of present-day disintegration. His instabilities are
partly those imposed by a decaying moral order, one which to the insecure—and Myers *was* insecure—afford no refuge. Human society is a

chaos at all times; and to evoke the stabilising capacities of 'tradition' is too frequently to forget the spasmodic efforts, involving rejections and false starts, instabilities and incoherences, which have gone to the formation of that tradition. Nevertheless the very eclecticism of Myers's work—its hovering between reason and intuition, between isolation and relationship, between subjectivist 'philosophy' and objectivist 'ethics', between a new social order and transcendental sanctions, between true self and social self, even between Eastern and Western modes of thought, to mention only a few—indicates how much to-day is demanded of the individual mind in ordering and integrating. Myers exemplifies—and, of course, he is not alone in doing this—the truth of Matthew Arnold's stress on both the man and the moment before great creativity is possible. His life would not have been easy even had he lived within a comparatively stable and coherent social order. The burden of so great a disintegration was too much for him. He indicates, indeed, how much further the breakdown of 'civilisation', of the civilising influence of the more self-conscious elements of society, had gone since the time of Henry James. But though to James 'Europe' presented possibilities of corruption as against the simpler verities of America, it also presented essential opportunities of 'experience' without which development was impossible. Myers finds no such possibilities among the self-conscious elements of his time. He feels all the time that growth can only come by remaining over against the 'society' (in the aristocratic sense) of his day; and he is thus led to regrettable, if perhaps inevitable over-simplifications. The fault lies partly in the further degeneration of 'society' since James's day; but also in Myers's inability to cope with, fundamentally to assimilate and assess impersonally, the corruption by which he himself felt surrounded.

Yet, what I have said here in evidence of his egotisms and his weaknesses must not be taken in a condemnatory or carping vein; it is intended to pay him the final compliment of quite impartial investigation. For, whatever criticisms are made, one matter remains clear: how much he deserves our gratitude for having accomplished so much.